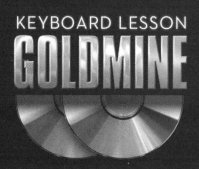

KEYBOARD LESSON
GOLDMINE

100

JAZZ LESSONS

BY PETER DENEFF & BRENT EDSTROM

ISBN 978-1-4803-5479-1

HAL•LEONARD®
CORPORATION

7777 W. BLUEMOUND RD. P.O. BOX 13819 MILWAUKEE, WI 53213

In Australia Contact:
Hal Leonard Australia Pty. Ltd.
4 Lentara Court
Cheltenham, Victoria, 3192 Australia
Email: ausadmin@halleonard.com.au

Visit Hal Leonard Online at
www.halleonard.com

CONTENTS

Lessons 1–40 by Peter Deneff

Lessons 41–90 by Brent Edstrom

ADVENTURES IN RHYTHM – CARRYING OVER THE BAR

Just as we can use harmony to create excitement and tension, we can also use rhythm to generate interesting ideas. The idea of "playing with the time" is commonplace in the percussion world. Many of the rhythmic devices used by percussionists can be applied to the piano as well. One of these concepts is the technique of **repeating a rhythmic phrase over the bar**. This is differs from the concept of "phrasing over the bar," which is the practice of starting a phrase in the middle of a bar and carrying through the bar line. Instead, this has to do with taking a phrase that doesn't fit evenly into a bar and repeating it over and over, starting on a different beat each time.

One of the most common ways of performing this is by repeating a three-beat phrase over a 4/4 bar. Notice how the phrase starts on beat 1, then 4, then 3, then 2, etc.

EXAMPLE 1

Similarly, one can create two- or four-bar phrases when playing in 3/4.

EXAMPLE 2

Try some odd phrasings.

EXAMPLE 3

It's also fun to play phrases containing smaller values like eighth notes or 16th notes.

EXAMPLE 4

When practicing these, try to maintain the 4/4 pulse in your mind while keeping the repeating phrase going. It is very important not to lose count.

LESSON #2: ADVENTURES IN RHYTHM – TRIPLETS

Triplets can be challenging to perform, but are an essential tool in an improviser's rhythmic toolbox. Triplets, being the most common tuplet, are a typical rhythm found in bebop phrasing.

EXAMPLE 1

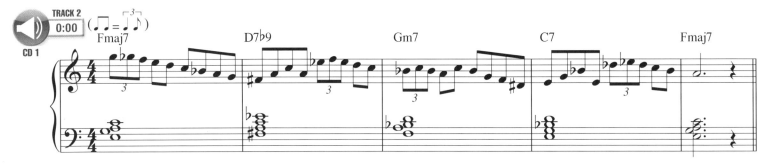

EXAMPLE 2

To practice interpreting triplets accurately, try playing the following scale exercise with a metronome.

You can try changing the note values; for instance, quarter, triplet, 16th, eighth, or any combination. Also, try to play all your major and minor scales in this manner for extra practice.

EXAMPLE 3

Continue in the same manner, playing triplets (three octaves) and 16th notes (four octaves), as demonstrated on Track 2.

Arpeggiated triads or other motives can be played using triplets and can provide tension and excitement to your solo.

EXAMPLE 4

Triplets can also be used to obscure the rhythm and carry over the bar. This can be done by phrasing the triplets in groups of four, for example.

EXAMPLE 5

In a Latin jazz style, alternating left- and right-hand chords can be played with triplets. Triplets must be performed accurately in order to be effective so make sure you always practice with a metronome.

EXAMPLE 6

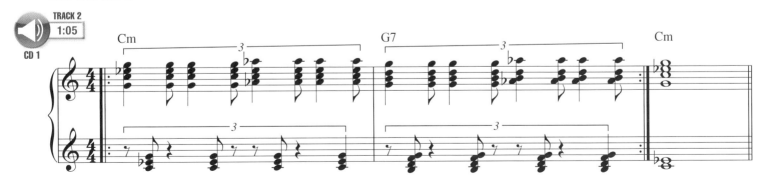

LESSON #3: ALTERED DOMININANT SCALE

Improvisers are constantly looking for new scales and sounds to play over jazz chord progressions. The more scales one has at their disposal, the more material they have to work with when improvising. Often, the scales are non-diatonic, that is, they are not based on the major scale or any of its modes. Such is the case with the **altered dominant scale**. This scale is usually played over an altered V or V7 chord.

EXAMPLE 1

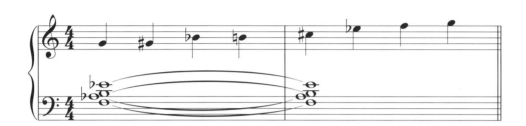

The scale is called "altered" because it contains a ♭9, ♯9, ♯11, and ♭13.

EXAMPLE 2

All scale tones do not need to be used and some interesting lines can be created because of this.

EXAMPLE 3

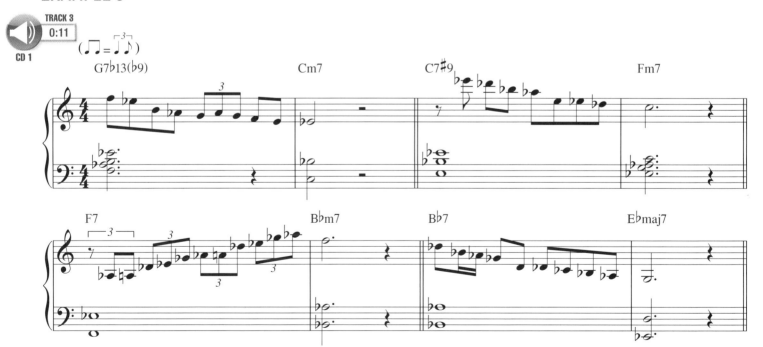

Play through the following lines. Pick your favorites and learn in 12 keys. Try to use the altered scale in your own improvisations on your favorite tunes.

EXAMPLE 4

TRACK 3
0:25
CD 1

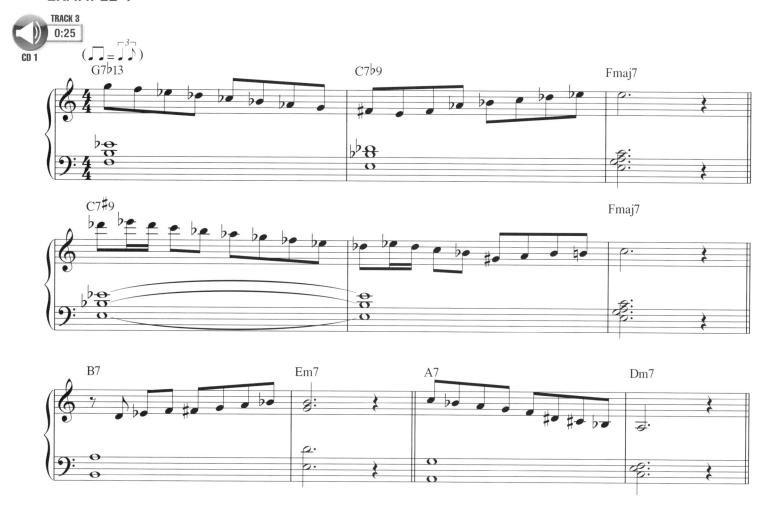

LESSON #4: ARPEGGIATING THROUGH THE CHANGES

The ability to navigate through the chord changes of a given tune is one of the most elemental skills a jazz improviser must develop. Even before one is able to create cohesive melodies over the harmonic structure, they must be able to conceptualize the form and chordal scheme. An effective way to approach this is simply to arpeggiate through the changes in time.

First, try to arpeggiate through the following passages using the scale tones 1, 3, 5, 7.

EXAMPLE 1

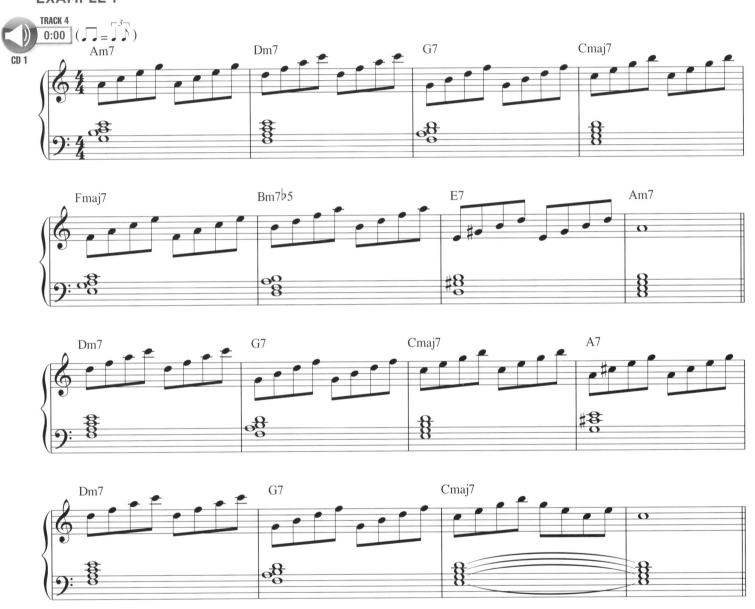

Next, let's try using the scale tones 3, 5, 7, 9.

EXAMPLE 2

Now play a combination of the two.

EXAMPLE 3

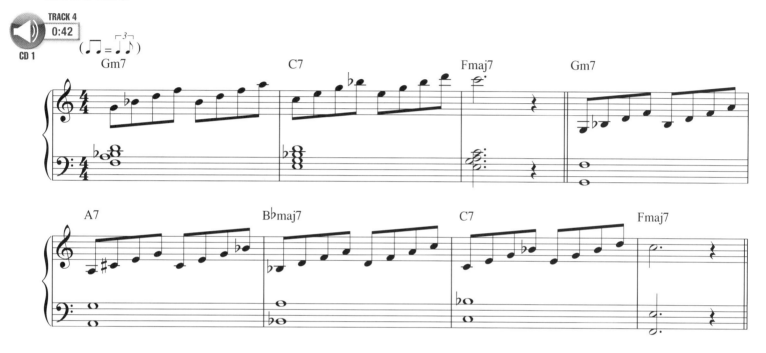

For an added challenge, we can try 16th notes and eighth-note triplets.

EXAMPLE 4

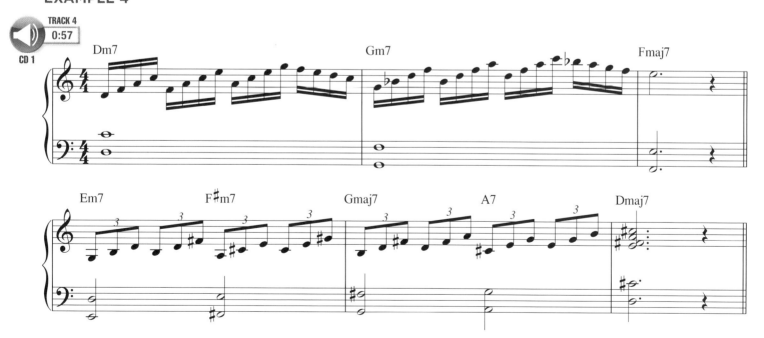

Try arpeggiating through your own favorite jazz tunes.

BILL EVANS VOICINGS

Bill Evans (1929–1980) was a great jazz pianist and an innovator in the style. His playing style has been studied and imitated by innumerable pianists over the past 50 years. Although Evans was a prolific composer and improviser, his left-hand comping style has always been of particular interest to jazz pianists. Pianists predating him had played similar voicings, but Evans codified the vocabulary of jazz piano harmony.

The voicings that Bill Evans put into common practice were essentially rootless 7th or 9th chords in first or third inversion.

They can be played in the right hand with the bass note in the left, solo piano style.

They can also be played in the left hand, leaving the right hand free to play melodic lines or colorful chord tones in the higher register.

EXAMPLE 1

EXAMPLE 2

EXAMPLE 3

The voicings need not contain all four tones (3, 5, 7, 9). Begin by practicing ii-V-I progressions using only the root, 3rd, and 7th.

Next try adding a 9th and 5th.

EXAMPLE 4

EXAMPLE 5

Lastly, add all four upper tones.

EXAMPLE 6

The voicings can be practiced in all keys by playing ii-V-I progressions in descending whole steps and descending half steps starting in both first inversion and third inversion. These voicings are an essential skill for the jazz pianist. Practice them diligently and thoroughly until they can be played effortlessly and rapidly.

DESCENDING WHOLE STEPS

DESCENDING HALF STEPS

LESSON #6: BRAZILIAN COMPING – BOSSA NOVA

The **bossa nova** (meaning "new trend" in Portuguese) music of Brazil in the 1950s left a greater impact on the jazz world than it did even in its own country. The swaying, gentle bossa rhythm has since become a mainstay in the standard vernacular of jazz players and composers. As in most Afro-based Latin rhythms, Brazilian music has a specific pulse or **clave** to it. This unique clave gives the rhythm its particular sound and phrasing. Without getting too far into specifics, most Latin rhythms are phrased in two bars: one being rhythmically consonant (downbeat oriented) and one being dissonant (upbeat oriented). The bossa nova piano rhythm is no exception.

There are two ways to play the bossa nova, each according to the clave. The first pattern is what one would play on a **forward clave**, that is, a clave with the rhythmically consonant bar preceding the dissonant one.

EXAMPLE 1

TRACK 6
0:00
CD 1

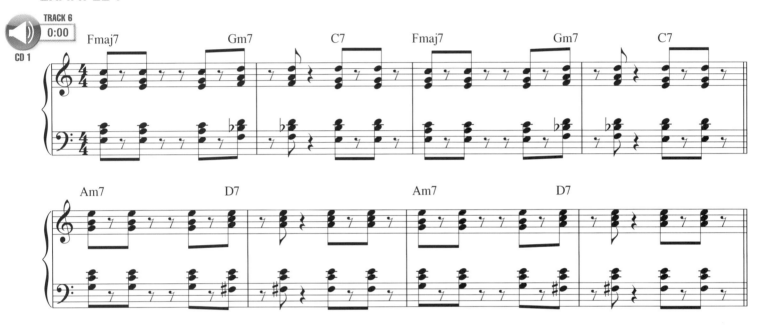

The other way to play this rhythm is according to the **reverse clave**, or the clave with the rhythmically dissonant bar preceding the consonant one.

EXAMPLE 2

TRACK 6
0:19
CD 1

The clave itself is usually established by the rhythm section and agreed upon by all members. Sometimes, an advanced group of Latin musicians might change the direction of the clave mid-song.

If one were to play the bossa groove on piano alone (sans bass), as to accompany a singer for instance, then the following patterns would be played.

EXAMPLE 3

TRACK 6
0:37
CD 1

LESSON #7: BRAZILIAN COMPING – SAMBA

The **samba**, bossa nova's older and more energetic sibling, is widely considered the national music and dance of Brazil and originated in the early part of the 20th century. Like bossa nova, samba, too, has a specific pulse or clave. The pulse of samba is similar to bossa in that it has a forward clave (consonant/dissonant) and reverse clave (dissonant/consonant). The major differences in the two rhythms are the tempo, samba being generally faster, and the specific parts that the percussion instruments play.

The following are examples of how to play a forward clave pattern.

EXAMPLE 1

TRACK 7
0:00
CD 1

Try these reverse clave patterns, notice the interesting effect of avoiding the downbeat on the first bar of the phrase.

EXAMPLE 2

TRACK 7
0:22
CD 1

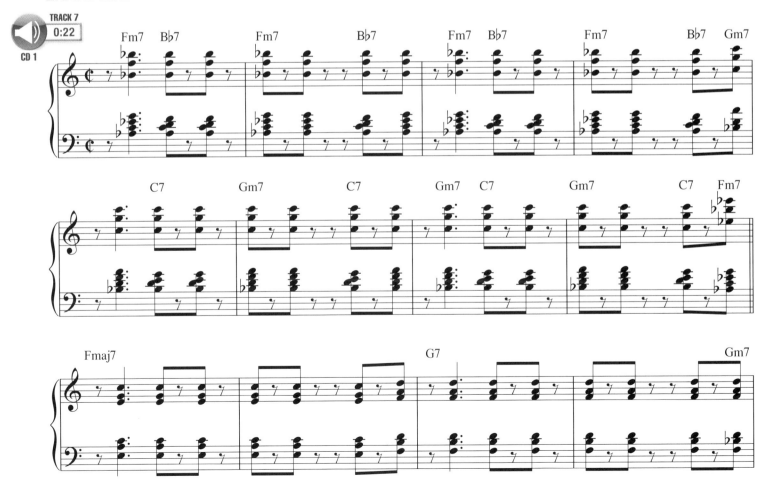

If one were to play these patterns solo piano with piano bass in the left hand, they would be performed in the following ways.

EXAMPLE 3

LESSON #8: BUILDING YOUR CHOPS

When it comes building your chops, or advancing your technical ability on the instrument, there is no substitute for some good old-fashioned practicing with a metronome. However, there are some specific ways that one can practice in order to build their speed and endurance.

Firstly, the use of a **metronome** is a must. Nowadays, there is no excuse not to use a metronome. While there are many digital models available, most of us already have metronomes built into an electronic keyboard or a smart phone. You can even access an Internet-based metronome on your computer.

The next step is to select your **practice material**. Let's try the bebop line below. Start with the metronome set to a reasonable tempo that allows you to execute the line perfectly, with no mistakes. Then, practice the line over and over, increasing the tempo by one increment only. If you play the line incorrectly, then you must decrease the tempo by one increment. As you practice in this manner, your speed will trend upward as your chops get better and faster.

EXAMPLE 1

You can use this technique to practice **voicings**.

EXAMPLE 2

Try it on some **scales**.

EXAMPLE 3

Now apply it to these **arpeggios**, or practically any piece of music you are working on.

EXAMPLE 4

TRACK 8
0:31
CD 1

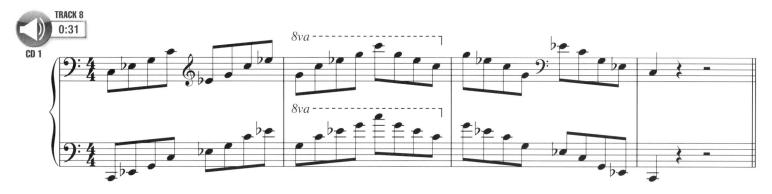

Try using this metronome technique on **Hanon exercises** or on the following jazz patterns.

EXAMPLE 5

TRACK 8
0:38
CD 1

LESSON #9: CHROMATICISM I

While chord tones and scales play an important role in crafting good jazz lines, it is the non-scalar or **chromatic** notes that provide the needed tension or color to a melody. In fact, the word "chromatic" itself is derived from the Greek word "chroma," which means color. When one speaks of the chromatic scale, they are referring to a succession of half steps.

EXAMPLE 1

TRACK 9
0:00
CD 1

Chromatic tones, on the other hand, can be described as any non-diatonic note.

EXAMPLE 2

TRACK 9
0:11
CD 1

Chromatic tones can be used as half-step approaches to scalar notes, either singly or in succession.

EXAMPLE 3

TRACK 9
0:20
CD 1

This is useful in creating interesting linear shapes and also in helping to time the resolution of the chord tones on strong harmonic beats.

EXAMPLE 4

TRACK 9
0:37
CD 1

Play through the following phrases that employ chromatic notes, then take your favorite phrases and learn them in all keys.

EXAMPLE 5

Try composing your own chromatic lines, keeping in mind that they should have good phrasing, interesting shape, and clear direction.

LESSON #10: CHROMATICISM II

Chromatic notes do not necessarily have to be played in succession. One can also apply chromatic techniques to harmonic shapes and arpeggiated passages. For instance, one can connect two adjacent chords through an intermediary chord, a half step between them.

EXAMPLE 1

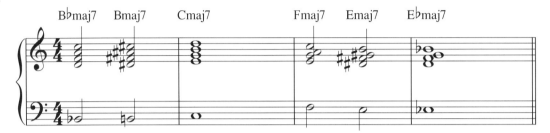

Additionally, as a tension-building effect, one can play parallel ascending chromatic chords over a bass pedal point.

EXAMPLE 2

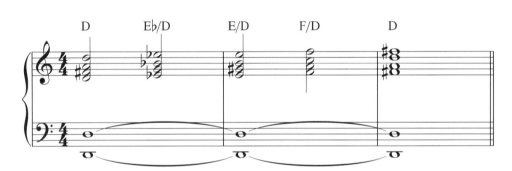

The concept of chromatic chords can be taken to another level through the use of arpeggiation. The following melodies are comprised of arpeggiated 7th chords.

EXAMPLE 3

For a more modern sound, one can arpeggiated chromatic ascending or descending suspended chords or quartal voicings.

EXAMPLE 4

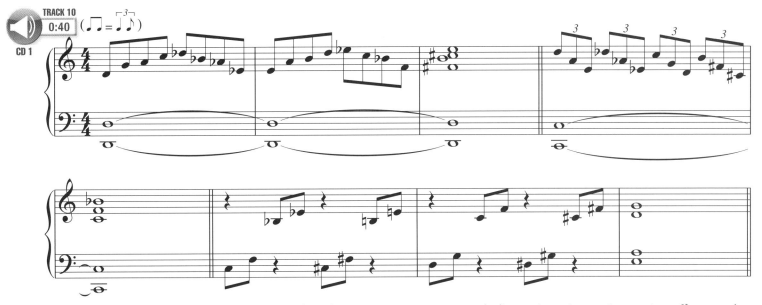

Besides simple arpeggiation, one can employ chromatic movement to melodic motives. A very interesting effect can be created simply by shifting a melody up or down by a half step.

EXAMPLE 5

One can also transpose a short motive in similar fashion.

EXAMPLE 6

Just as Brazilian music has had a long-lasting influence on the world of jazz, Cuban music has left its unique impact as well. One of the most popular rhythms in this genre is the **cha-cha**, which is a slow-to-medium tempo dance in 4/4. There are a couple of ways to comp over a cha-cha groove. Since the cha-cha rhythm is phrased in two bars, the piano accompaniment is phrased accordingly. The first bar starts on the downbeat and the second bar begins on the "and" of one. Play through the following idiomatic cha-cha progressions using full block chords in both hands.

EXAMPLE 1

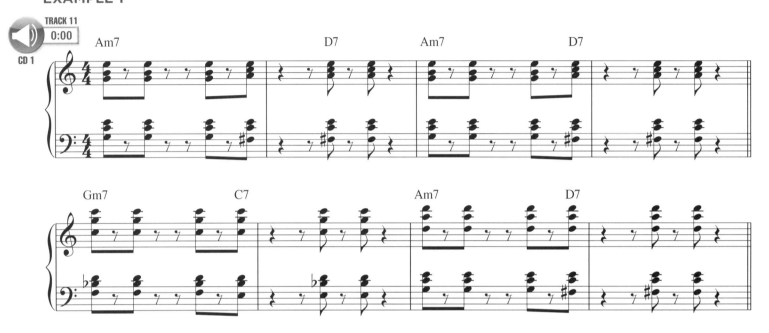

Sometimes the pianist might play a chordal accompaniment in the following fashion.

EXAMPLE 2

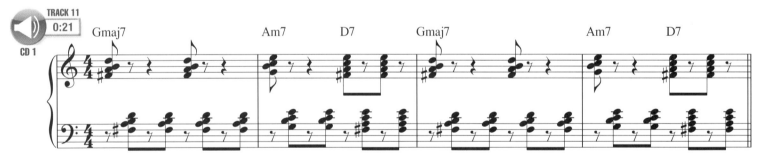

The other way to accompany a cha-cha is by playing a **montuno** pattern (a typical Cuban piano pattern consisting of alternating octaves and block or broken chords). These are some standard montunos that one would play, using octaves and block chords. The CD track includes five examples. The first two are shown here.

EXAMPLE 3

For variation, one can choose to play broken chords rather than block chords, or a combination of the two. Here are some commonly used montunos. The CD track includes three examples. The first two are shown here.

EXAMPLE 4

If one were to play these without a bass player, the pianist can perform the bass function using their left hand. The CD track includes two examples. The first is given below.

EXAMPLE 5

As with any style, the best way to learn is by listening to great musicians within that genre. Make sure to listen to some great Latin jazz recordings so that you can learn the feel of the style, not just the notes.

LESSON #12:

CUBAN MONTUNOS – MAMBO PATTERNS

Another popular Cuban dance rhythm that has been adopted into the jazz vernacular is the **mambo**. The mambo is an up-tempo rhythm originating from the Cuban *Son* in the early decades of the 20th century. The pulse of the mambo, like many Latin styles, is the clave. There are two types of claves in the mambo: the forward clave and the reverse clave. The clave determines which bar of the two-bar phrase gets the heavier downbeat. This will affect how the players interpret the groove.

EXAMPLE 1

As in the cha-cha, montunos or block chords can be used in the piano accompaniment of the mambo. Here are some examples of chordal comping.

EXAMPLE 2

Montunos with block chords can be played as well. Here are various typical patterns.

EXAMPLE 3

TRACK 12
0:35
CD 1

Arpeggiated montunos are also common, stylistically. Try playing through these various idiomatic progressions.

EXAMPLE 4

TRACK 12
0:48
CD 1

Latin jazz is a lot of fun to play and can be a welcome challenge for the jazz student. Try these patterns over your own chord changes and make sure to listen to the great artists of the style for inspiration.

Diminished scales are octatonic (eight notes) and are comprised of alternating whole and half steps.

EXAMPLE 1

This arrangement of notes creates a sound that is dissonant, yet approachable. The scale works well over diminished triads, half diminished 7ths, fully diminished 7ths, dominant 7th, and altered dominant chords.

EXAMPLE 2

When played over a dominant chord, the scale creates a ♭9, ♯9, and ♯11, which gives it an altered quality. By omitting certain scale tones, interesting melodic combinations can be created.

EXAMPLE 3

The scale works particularly well in minor mode and can be combined with the harmonic minor scale.

EXAMPLE 4

Play through the following examples and learn your favorites in as many keys as you can.

EXAMPLE 5

DOMINANT CYCLE PROGRESSION

One of the most common harmonic movements in jazz, besides the ii-V-I, is the **dominant cycle** – otherwise known as the **Circle of 5ths** – harmonized as 7th chords. The dominant cycle inherently creates some interesting voice-leading movements. For one thing, there is the bass movement, which can descend a 4th and ascend a 5th, or vice-versa.

EXAMPLE 1

The other movement that is worth mentioning is the chromatic descent of the 3rd and 7th.

EXAMPLE 2

As a voicings exercise, the progression should be practiced the following ways, starting with the essential root, 3rd, and 7th, and then gradually adding the 5ths and 9ths.

EXAMPLE 3

Then it can be practiced voiced in alternating 13ths and ♭9ths or ♭13th and 9ths.

Melodically, one can practice playing sequential lines over the progression. By design, it will take you through all 12 keys.

EXAMPLE 4

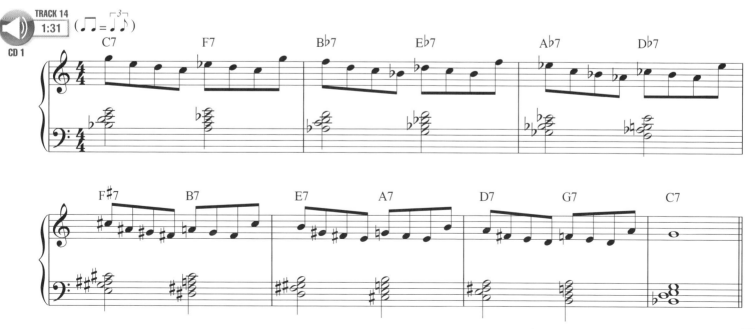

LESSON #15: EXOTIC SCALES

Most Western musicians are familiar with the major and minor scales and their modes. Even the pentatonic and blues scales are fairly well known, especially to jazz musicians. Even though these scales represent a great deal of material when learned in 12 keys, they are only a fraction of scalar world.

There are countless scales in use, including many that go beyond the limits of our Western equal-tempered 12-tone scale.

These exotic scales can be very useful to the jazz improviser, especially the improviser of so-called "world music." One such scale is the **Mixolydian ♭2♭6 scale**, also known as the **Phrygian dominant scale**, or the **hijaz scale**. This scale contains an augmented 2nd between the 2nd and 3rd scale degrees and is based on the 5th degree of the harmonic minor scale.

EXAMPLE 1

TRACK 15 0:00 CD 1

Another interesting scale is the **sus4 pentatonic**. It is tonally ambiguous and very useful as a jazz scale. It works well over quartal voicings.

EXAMPLE 2

TRACK 15 0:15 CD 1

Another closely related scale is the **sus4 ♭2 pentatonic**. It can be used over a Phrygian passage as well as over dominant chords.

EXAMPLE 2

TRACK 15 0:21 CD 1

The last scale we will look at is the **Phrygian dim4 scale**. This scale has the unique feature of having a minor 3rd as well as a diminished 4th (enharmonic major 3rd). It sounds especially good over a dominant 7♯9 chord.

EXAMPLE 3

TRACK 15
0:35
CD 1

There are many more scales in the world than could ever be contained in one volume, much less in one lesson. Learn as many of them as you can and find ways to implement them into your own music.

LESSON #16: FUNKY COMPING

When playing jazz-funk, the keyboardist is often required to play rhythmic patterns, not unlike those of a rhythm guitar player, bass player, or both simultaneously. These patterns are typically played on the piano, electric piano, organ, and especially the **Clavinet**. Most **funky patterns** are based on a repetitive vamp and are usually syncopated between the hands. Here are some simple patterns to start with. It is essential to practice these with a metronome, drum machine, or perhaps even a real drummer – if they have good rhythm, of course.

EXAMPLE 1

The following patterns are based on 16th-note grooves and are a bit more challenging. They would typically be played with a more percussive keyboard sound like a Clavinet. Notice that these patterns are handy exercises for the left hand.

EXAMPLE 2

Finally, here are some more exercises using typical voicings and patterns.

EXAMPLE 3

TRACK 16
0:50
CD 1

LESSON #17: GOSPEL CHORDS

The gospel piano sound has its own history and development that is related to but quite independent from the development of jazz piano. While one could write volumes on the stylistic techniques of **gospel music**, this chapter will concentrate on one of its most common devices, descending three-note chords over a pedal point. Gospel music tends to favor IV-I harmonic movement.

EXAMPLE 1

TRACK 17
0:00
CD 1

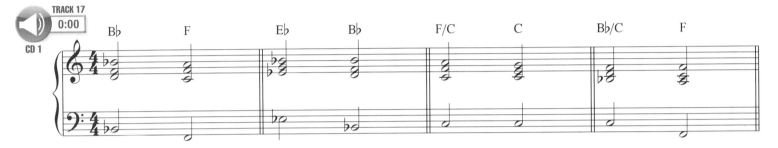

Such harmonic movement is probably due to the ecclesiastical nature of the style, with plagal cadences (IV-I) being abundant in many forms of church music. This plagal movement can be heard in many examples of gospel progressions and as the final "Amen" at the end of countless hymns. Try playing these simple vamps. Notice the voice-leading movement.

EXAMPLE 2

TRACK 17
0:21
CD 1

This movement can be applied to longer chordal phrases. Play through the following examples.

EXAMPLE 3

LESSON #18: LATIN IMPROV IDEAS I

The original performers of Latin jazz were essentially bebop players and Latin players. When these pioneers improvised, they did so using the jazz vocabulary that they were accustomed to. In fact, it has become quite standard to play bebop lines over Latin jazz tunes, with straight eighths, of course. However, since the early days, Latin jazz piano players have incorporated certain techniques and motives into their solos that are specifically Latin, not just borrowed from straight-ahead jazz.

It might be that early Latin jazz players needed to play octaves for the sake of being able to compete volume-wise with the percussion section, amplified bass, and brass. Whatever the cause of its inception was, octave passages have become standard fare for the Latin pianist. In order to start developing your octave technique, try playing through the following scales, hands alone as well as together.

EXAMPLE 1

TRACK 18
0:00
CD 1

Here are some other typical octave lines that should be practiced.

EXAMPLE 2

TRACK 18
0:15
CD 1

The hands can be placed a 3rd apart, playing harmonized octaves.

EXAMPLE 3

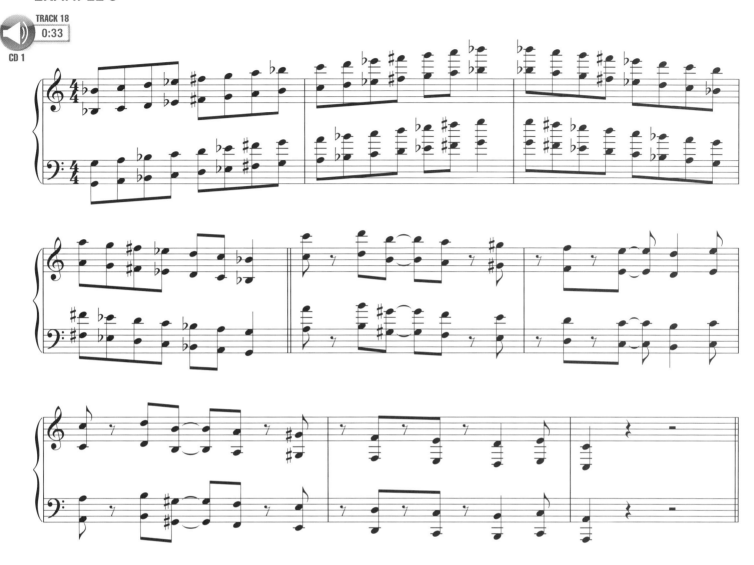

Syncopated lines and patterns can be created using octaves and chords, similar to what a percussionist might play.

EXAMPLE 4

LATIN IMPROV IDEAS II

Other ideas that are idiomatic in Latin jazz are repeated passages such as the following. The CD track includes four examples. The first three are shown here.

EXAMPLE 1

TRACK 19
0:00
CD 1

Harmonized lines in 3rds are also commonly used in the style. The lines often contain arpeggios and scalar passages. The CD track includes four examples. The first two are shown here.

EXAMPLE 2

TRACK 19
0:29
CD 1

Rhythmic and syncopated figures can be played using chords in both hands. Notice the Latin effect of the syncopation.

EXAMPLE 3

Using arpeggiated or non-arpeggiated chords, one can also create some interesting rhythmic effects. The ideas actually are a variation on the concept of the montuno and can be played in many ways. The CD track includes six examples. The first two are shown here.

EXAMPLE 4

The CD includes three examples of patterns with the hands placed a 10th apart. The first one is shown below.

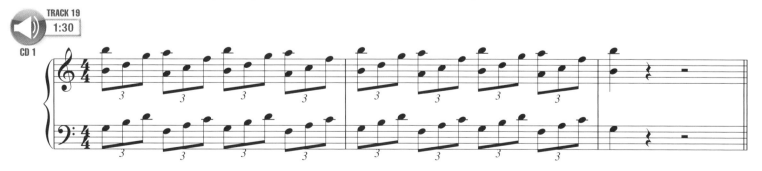

Because Latin improvisations are commonly played over a single vamp, the pianist has a great deal of freedom to superimpose different rhythms and harmonies over the static harmony.

LESSON #20: LATIN JAZZ – AFRO-CUBAN 6/8

While the genre of Latin jazz has many interesting and contagious rhythms, one of the most unique – and in fact, most rooted in its African heritage – is the **Afro-Cuban 6/8**. This groove, like many African-based Latin rhythms, has a clave as its heartbeat. This clave is a one-bar phrase that sets the emphasized pulse of the music. The first three beats are rhythmically consonant and the last three beats are instable or dissonant.

EXAMPLE 1

Here are some ways a pianist might comp to the Afro-Cuban 6/8, using two-handed voicing and left hand bass accompaniment.

EXAMPLE 2

Creating lines in 6/8 can be challenging for a performer accustomed to playing primarily in 4/4, but one can conceptualize in terms of how to phrase triplets in duple meter.

EXAMPLE 3

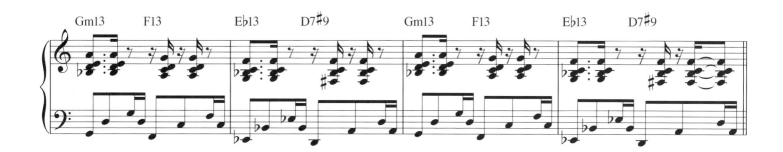

Play through the following 6/8 lines. Notice that the first one is tonal and the second one is modal, just as one might expect from Afro-Cuban jazz.

EXAMPLE 4

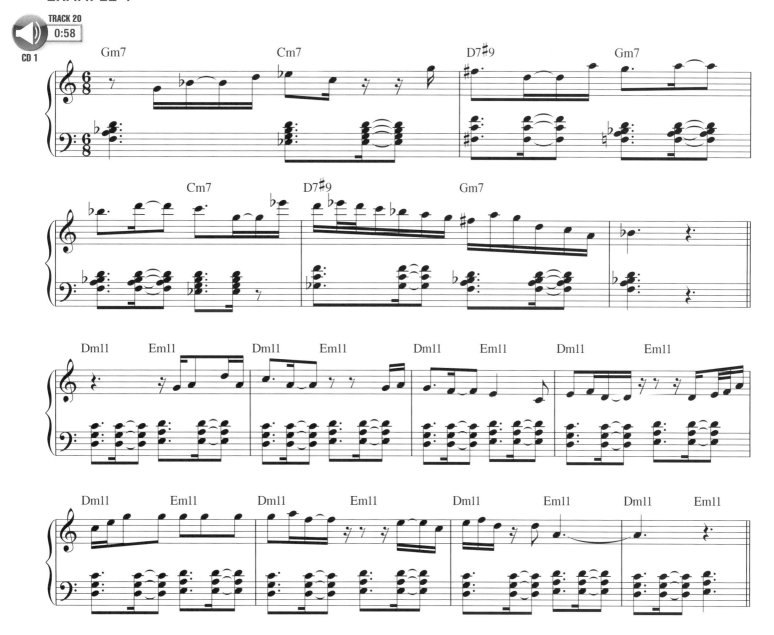

LATIN STRIDE PATTERNS

The techniques of stride piano, otherwise known as the bass-chord function, can be applied to other styles of music in creative ways. Take, for example, the rhythms of Latin music. In many cases, these rhythms can be played by the left hand in a stride-like style.

The **rhumba** is a fairly simple rhythm to play, using a single note bass and triadic chords.

EXAMPLE 1

TRACK 21
0:00
CD 1

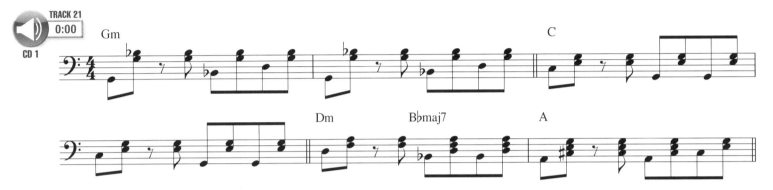

A **bossa nova** is also possible to orchestrate in the same way.

EXAMPLE 2

TRACK 21
0:21
CD 1

The bossa can also be played with an octave bass.

EXAMPLE 3

TRACK 21
0:31
CD 1

Perhaps the most challenging pattern to master is **Cuban stride**. It is highly syncopated and never falls on beat one except on the initial downbeat. It maintains the *tumbao* bass line while concurrently keeping an accompaniment-chord pattern. Play through the Cuban stride patterns in Example 4.

EXAMPLE 4

TRACK 21
0:41

CD 1

The following measures include patterns in the right hand.

EXAMPLE 5

TRACK 21
1:05

CD 1

Try your own patterns and ultimately add improvised lines over the left-hand pattern.

LESSON #22: LEFT-HAND STRIDE TECHNIQUE

Stride piano came out of the tradition of ragtime, but the concept of the stride pattern can be traced back to European parlor music of the 1800s or even earlier. The function of the **stride pattern** is two-fold: 1) it provides the bass function; 2) it also serves as the chordal harmony. One kind of stride pattern contains a single bass note on beats 1 and 3 and a two- or three-note chord on beats 2 and 4. In earlier styles, the chords might be rather simple and triadic.

EXAMPLE 1

TRACK 22
0:00
CD 1

In later styles, the harmony can be played using more 7ths, 9ths, or 13ths.

EXAMPLE 2

TRACK 22
0:19
CD 1

A more challenging way to play the stride accompaniment is using an octave bass rather than single notes. Practice these examples slowly at first, gradually building up speed and endurance. Try adding a simple, repetitive pattern in the right hand.

EXAMPLE 3

TRACK 22
0:37
CD 1

You can also try to play runs and arpeggios with your right hand while maintaining the stride pattern in your left.

EXAMPLE 4

One of the first things many jazz players learn to play is the minor pentatonic or **blues scale**.

EXAMPLE 1

While these scales are a good starting place for improvisation, and quite versatile, they are not the only blues scales one can use. The other blues scale that is commonly used over dominant 7th chords is the **major blues scale**.

EXAMPLE 2

Upon first glance, one will notice that the scale contains the 1, 2, ♭3, 3, 5, and 6 scale degrees. But upon closer examination, one would discover that the notes of the major blues scale are exactly the same as the **relative minor blues scale**.

EXAMPLE 3

Sometimes the ♭6 interval can be added as it leads nicely from 5 to 6.

EXAMPLE 4

Play through the following examples and learn your favorites in all keys.

EXAMPLE 5

TRACK 23
0:31
CD 1

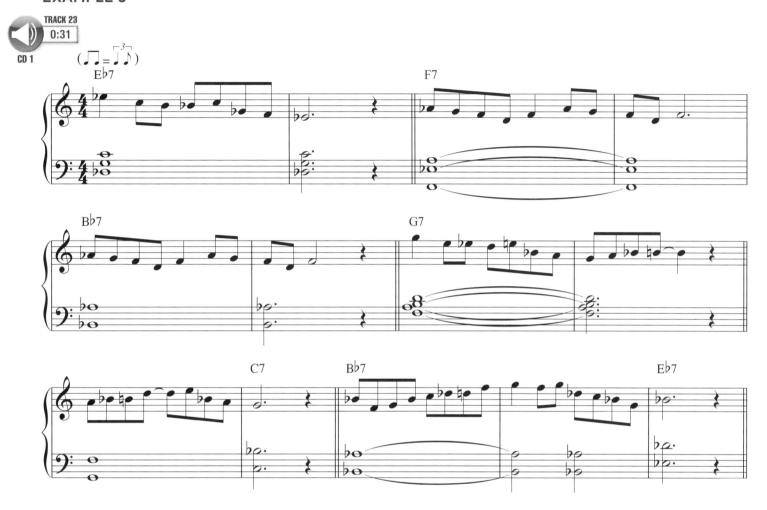

The major blues scale can be used in many types of music but is especially appropriate in blues, New Orleans, and even many folk styles.

LESSON #24: MELODIC CONTOUR

The concept of **melodic contour** is not unique to jazz. In fact, composers since the origins of musical development have aspired to create interesting and memorable melodies. One finds the evidence of purposeful melodic composing in the works of the ancient Greeks, early chant, Hildegard von Bingen, and J.S. Bach, all the way through Stravinsky, Bartók, Gershwin, and Thelonious Monk. Therefore, when improvising jazz lines, it is equally important to create melodic shapes that are interesting to the ear. While the most efficient way from point A to point B is a straight line, it is certainly not always the most interesting.

EXAMPLE 1

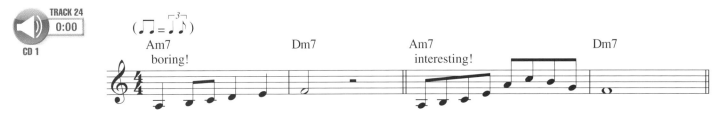

If one were to examine the jazz lines of one of the greats, like Charlie Parker, Bud Powell, or Chick Corea, one would notice that their melodies had direction, clear phrasing, and interesting shape.

EXAMPLE 2

The contour of the melody can be shaped through the use of directional variation and the employment of diatonic and chromatic scales, arpeggios, and larger intervals. Here are some passages that employ ascending and descending scalar (diatonic and chromatic) motion.

EXAMPLE 3

The following short phrases use only 3rds or larger intervals.

EXAMPLE 4

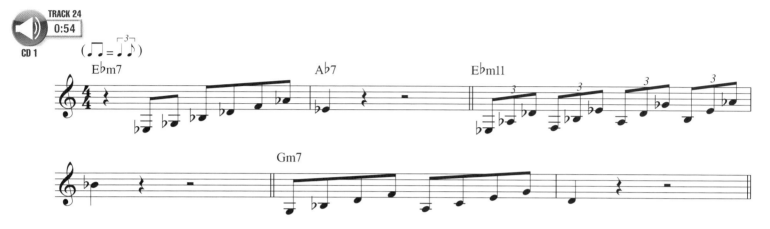

Finally, these lines are a combination of scales and larger intervals.

EXAMPLE 5

When crafting your own lines, make sure they have purpose, direction, and a pleasing melodic contour.

LESSON #25: MELODIC SEQUENCE

The concept of sequential movement has been a mainstay of compositional technique since the origins of music. The human ear likes familiarity, yet tires easily of repetition. **Sequence** is a way that musical material can be repeated and developed, without the risk of redundancy.

EXAMPLE 1

The melodies of many popular jazz standards are, in fact, sequences. Sequential movement can occur at any interval desired. Sequences of 2nds and 4ths are very common, but 3rds can be used as well.

EXAMPLE 2

There are two kinds of sequences: tonal and real. **Tonal sequences** are ones where the material is repeated by scalar movement, not chromatic modulation. The melodic intervals are modified according to the key signature.

EXAMPLE 3

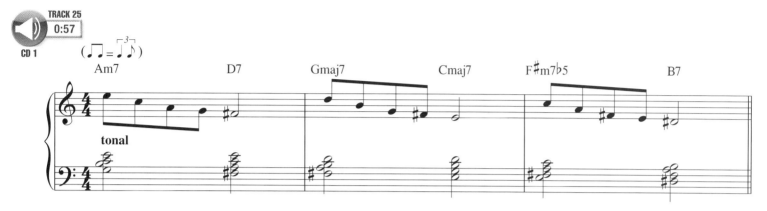

Real sequences are ones where the material is literally restated at a different interval. The relationships between the notes of the melody are not altered to maintain the tonality.

EXAMPLE 4

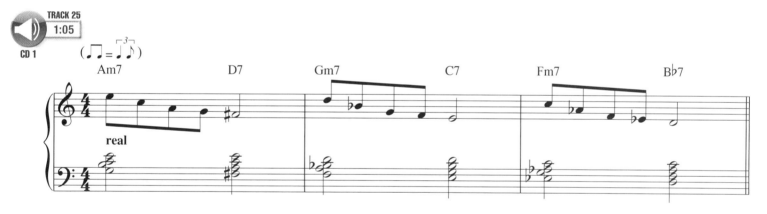

Sequence is an effective way to introduce and quickly familiarize new material to the listener.

The minor **ii°-V-i** is one of the most common progressions in jazz. One will find it, or a portion of it, in practically every jazz composition in the standard repertoire. It makes sense, then, to practice improvising melodic ideas over it. There are several scales that can be used over some or all of this progression: harmonic minor, melodic minor, natural minor, diminished scale, altered dominant scale, minor blues scale, and others.

EXAMPLE 1

Combining these scales with typical jazz melodic devices, one can come up with some very interesting lines. Notice the use of chromaticism to connect the scalar tones.

EXAMPLE 2

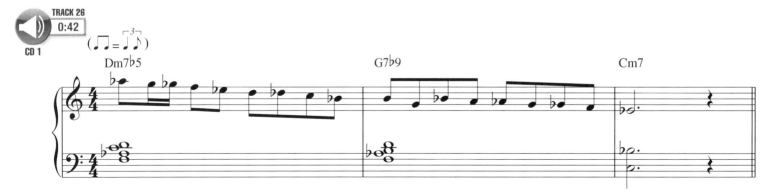

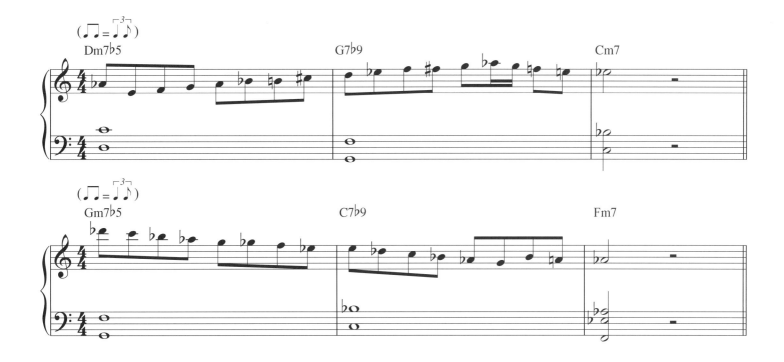

The following lines are a bit more modern and less bebop sounding.

EXAMPLE 3

TRACK 26
1:05
CD 1

One can create a more modern sound by outlining alternate chords in the melody, pentatonics, and quartal chord voicings.

EXAMPLE 4

TRACK 26
1:13
CD 1

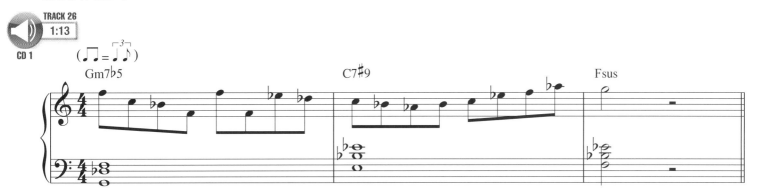

Take your favorite lines and learn them in 12 keys. Compose and improvise your own lines over this progression.

MOTIVES AND THEIR DEVELOPMENT

One of the characterizing elements of Western music is the concept of **motivic development**. Having its origins in the early centuries of European musical tradition, these compositional techniques have been inherited into the world of jazz composers and improvisers. Embellishing a simple melody in various ways is one of the easiest means to develop material.

EXAMPLE 1

TRACK 27
0:00
CD 1

Find your own ways to elaborate on this motive.

Another common technique is to change direction or invert the intervals of the line. There are three ways to alter the melody in this way: **retrograde** (playing it backward), **inversion** (upside-down), and **retrograde inversion** (backward and upside-down).

EXAMPLE 2

TRACK 27
0:25
CD 1

Sequence is another way to develop material. It is discussed in detail in Lesson 25, but essentially involves restating the melody at a different interval, either tonally or literally (real sequence).

EXAMPLE 3

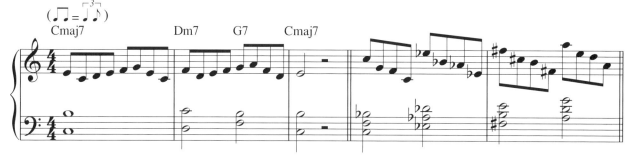

One can also alter a motive by **changing the mode** – for instance, major to minor or vice-versa. One could also adapt the motive to another non-Western mode.

EXAMPLE 4

Beyond harmonic or melodic devices, motives can also be developed by **changing the rhythm**. For instance, a melody can be displaced rhythmically or played over the bar.

EXAMPLE 5

Also, one can **alter the note values** – for instance, from quarter notes to triplets, eighths, or half notes.

EXAMPLE 6

Discover all the different ways you can expand your melodic ideas. This will add cohesiveness and interest to your improvisation and take you to new heights of creativity.

LESSON #28: ODD METER

Most jazz musicians are quite at home performing repertoire in conventional time signatures like 4/4, 3/4, and 6/8, but when it comes to **odd meters** like 5/8, 7/8, or 9/8, many of them don't feel as comfortable. This is not the case in other parts of the world, such as Greece or the Balkans, where odd meter is part of the general musical landscape.

Like all other musical skills, odd meters must be practiced in order to make them feel natural and flowing. Try practicing the following grooves until they seem natural. When you are at ease with them, you should be able to feel the rhythm, without having to count it.

EXAMPLE 1

TRACK 28
0:00
CD 1

The following passage is in 5/4. It includes left-hand accompaniment and an improvised line in the right.

EXAMPLE 2

TRACK 28
0:53
CD 1

It is especially challenging to solo over odd meters. This example is in 7/8 with a left-hand accompaniment and quick improvised lines in the right.

EXAMPLE 3

TRACK 28
1:11
CD 1

When interpreting odd meters, it is often helpful to count them in smaller groups of twos and threes. For instance, 5/8 can be 2 + 3 or 3 + 2. 9/8 can be counted as 3 + 3 + 3, 2 + 2 + 2 + 3, 3 + 2 + 2 + 2, 2 + 3 + 2 + 2, or 2 + 2 + 3 + 2.

LESSON #29: ORCHESTRATING TWO-HANDED VOICINGS

Jazz piano voicings can be a challenge for the novice. Just learning the basics with one hand can take many hours of practice and patience. However, what does one do with the right hand when a comping situation necessitates a two-handed chordal approach?

Approaching the orchestration, or voicing, of the chords with both hands is not unlike approaching the orchestration of an ensemble. In your low to mid register, you should play the substantial notes of the voicing – in other words, all the essential notes that must be played. The lower mid register sounds warm and full. Play your "Bill Evans" voicings with your left hand in this register.

EXAMPLE 1

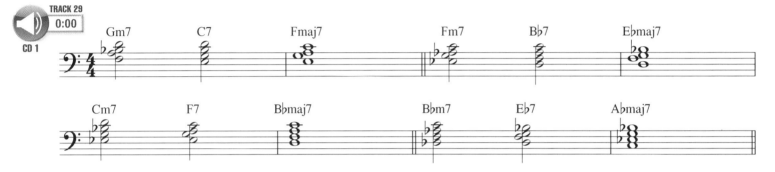

With your right hand, add notes to color the fundamental harmony. Accent the chord with octaves.

EXAMPLE 2

Try adding octaves and 4ths or 5ths for a bigger, more complex sound.

EXAMPLE 3

Triadic voicings can also be added in the right hand, as in Example 4. Finally, try playing quartal harmonies in your left hand, and 3rds or 4ths in the right hand, as shown in Example 5.

EXAMPLE 4

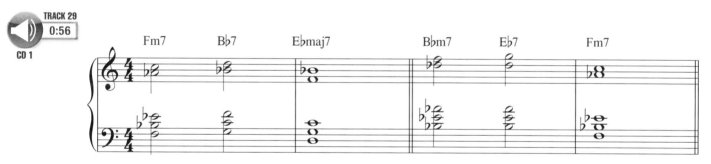

EXAMPLE 5

Don't be afraid to experiment and try new things. Let your ear be your guide.

LESSON #30: PHRYGIAN SOLO IDEAS

The **Phrygian scale** has been a favorite of composers in many genres, including jazz, classical, and world music. Its "Spanish flamenco" sound has been exploited by many composers and improvisers through the decades. The scale itself is based on E to E, all natural notes, or the scale formula H-W-W-W-H-W-W.

EXAMPLE 1

TRACK 30
0:00
CD 1

The following lines are based exclusively on the notes of the Phrygian scale given above.

EXAMPLE 2

TRACK 30
0:16
CD 1

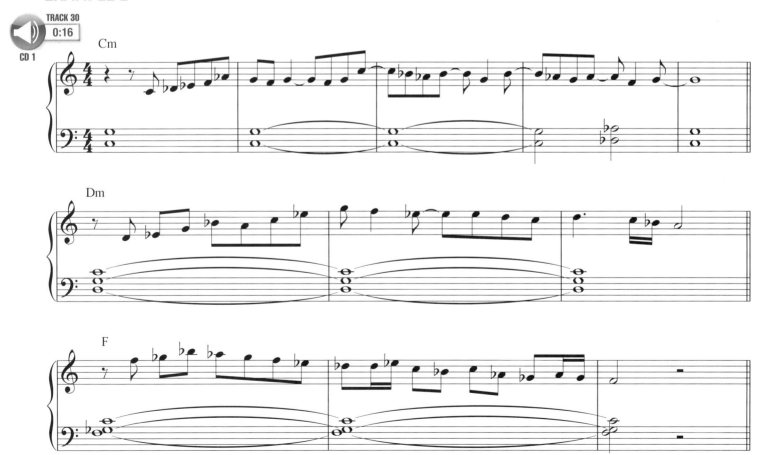

Playing the scalar notes unaltered can be rather limiting, and possibly monotonous, so we can introduce **chromaticism** into the lines. This adds interest and needed dissonance into our improvisation.

EXAMPLE 3

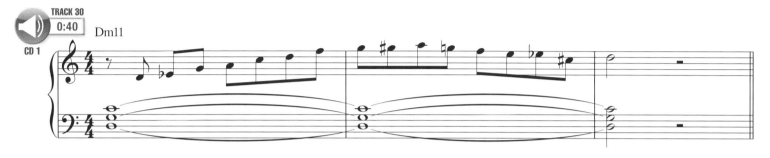

Keep in mind, however, that there is no V-I cadence in modal music, so the lines are devoid of this particular cadential impetus. We must maintain the interest, therefore, through the crafting of good melodic and directional lines. Here are some two-handed voicings that sound great in Phrygian mode.

EXAMPLE 4

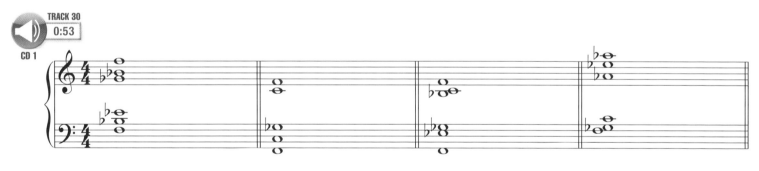

LESSON #31: PRACTICING THE MODES IN EVERY KEY

Learning the modes of the major scale is useful, particularly if one wants to improvise over a modal composition. However, it is equally important to be able to navigate through these modes for the purposes of playing tonal jazz. In that regard, it is important to practice these scales with their key center in mind. In other words, E to E might incidentally be "E Phrygian" in a modal context, but E to E still belongs to the key center of C major and should be viewed that way within a tonal context.

EXAMPLE 1

TRACK 31
0:00
CD 1

Practice the following exercise with the metronome. When you are able to execute it in 12 keys, your command of the keys and modes will be greatly increased.

EXAMPLE 2

TRACK 31
0:10
CD 1

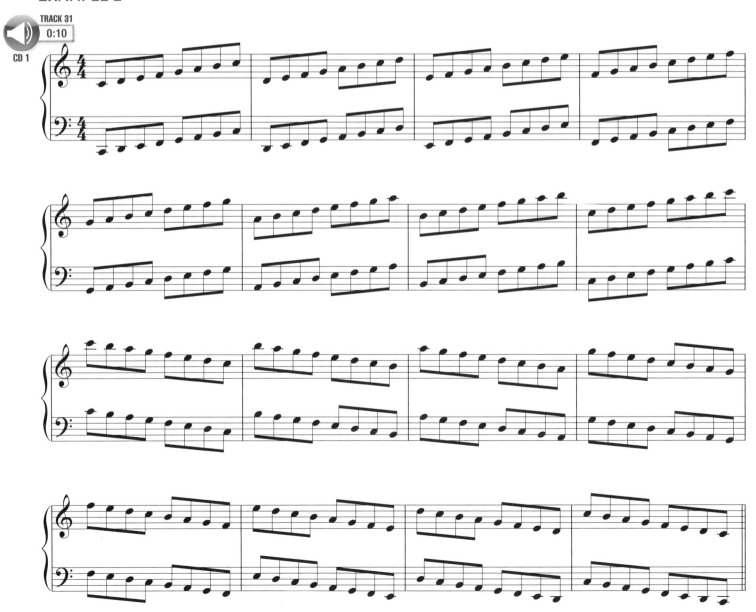

When you have mastered Example 2, you can try the following one.

EXAMPLE 3

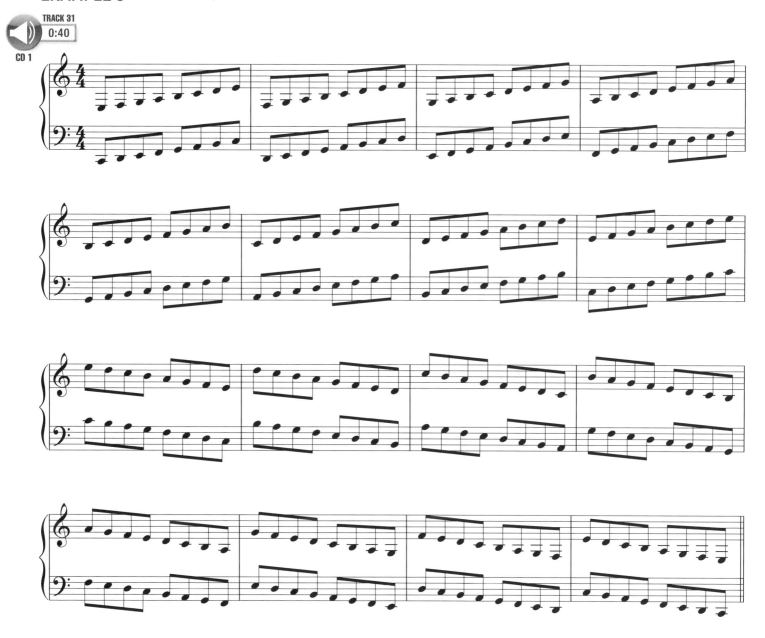

REHARMONIZATION

The concept of **reharmonization** has been around in some form since the early days of Western harmonic development and had really taken a stronghold by the Baroque era. Naturally, jazz composers were keen to apply this technique to their own music. The reharmonization of a melody can run from a simple chord substitution to a complete harmonic overhaul.

One way to reharmonize is by using borrowed chords from the parallel mode.

EXAMPLE 1

TRACK 32
0:00
CD 1

Also, one can substitute various chords with other diatonic chords, such as ii for IV, iv for I, or iii for V, or vise-versa.

EXAMPLE 2

TRACK 32
0:25
CD 1

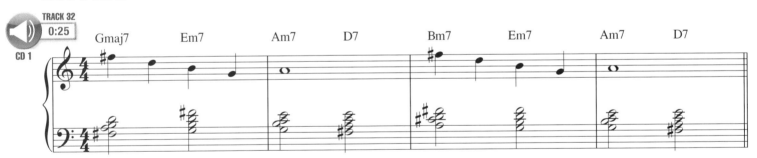

Furthermore, non-diatonic III/iii and IV/iv or ♭III/♭iii and ♭IV/♭iv chords can be used.

EXAMPLE 3

TRACK 32
0:38
CD 1

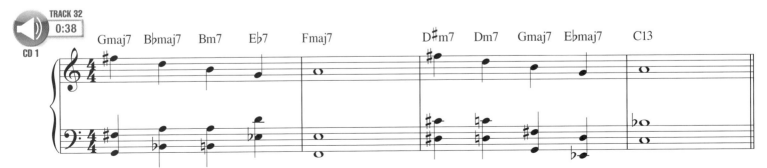

Secondary dominants and other secondary chords can be used, as well as any chromatic chord with the melody note as a primary chord tone or extension.

EXAMPLE 4

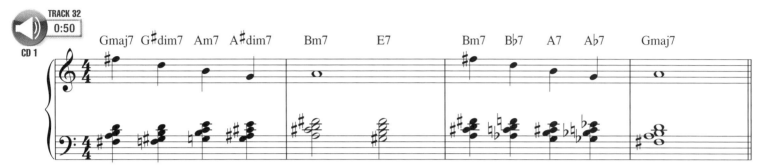

Play through the following example of "Ode to Joy" by Beethoven. It starts off with a simple harmony and then is reharmonized in the above-mentioned ways.

EXAMPLE 5

Try to reharmonize your own melodies using the preceding devices. Let your ear and musicality guide you through your harmonic adventure.

RHAPSODIC ADVENTURES – LONG MELODIC RUNS

In the world of jazz piano greats, there are several performers who generate much excitement due to their rhapsodic and classically inspired runs. Many of these musicians' lines appear to have more in common with Chopin or Rachmaninoff than Parker or Gillespie. In fact, many of these lines are directly borrowed from the classical piano repertoire.

One such line, which is very useful because it can be played over a dominant chord, is the fully diminished 7th run.

EXAMPLE 1

TRACK 33
0:00
CD 1

The following phrases incorporate the run into a jazz line.

EXAMPLE 2

TRACK 33
0:19
CD 1

Another run, which was made popular by Art Tatum, is the major or minor 6th run.

EXAMPLE 3

TRACK 33
0:34
CD 1

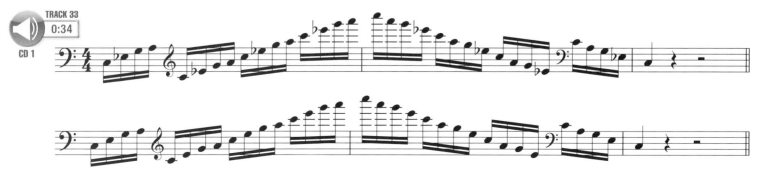

Similarly, any 7th chord can be played the same way.

EXAMPLE 4

TRACK 33
0:50
CD 1

Finally, there is the chromatic run.

EXAMPLE 5

TRACK 33
1:19
CD 1

Play through the following examples of chromatic runs, inspired by Bud Powell.

EXAMPLE 6

TRACK 33
1:31
CD 1

For other ideas, check out romantic piano literature by Liszt, Chopin, Rachmaninoff, et al and incorporate their lines into your own music.

LESSON #34: SECONDARY LEADING TONES

Jazz improvisers craft melodic lines using chord tones, scalar tones, and chromatic notes. By combining these notes, one can create virtually unlimited variations of interesting lines. One type of chromatic note that is frequently used is the **secondary leading tone** (SLT). SLTs are non-scale tones that are a half step below any scalar note.

EXAMPLE 1

They are often used in conjunction with primary leading tones as well as naturally occurring SLTs like the second scale degree in minor or the third scale degree in major.

EXAMPLE 2

They lead quite naturally upward into the scale tone that they are tonicizing; however, they don't necessarily need to be used in that way. SLTs can help to create tension.

EXAMPLE 3

They can provide interesting linear contour.

EXAMPLE 4

SLTs can lengthen or delay the termination of the line.

EXAMPLE 5

SLTs can also be used to create motivic development such as sequential movement.

EXAMPLE 6

Play through the following lines and choose your favorite ideas to learn in 12 keys and incorporate into your own playing!

EXAMPLE 7

LESSON #35: TAKING IT OUT – CHROMATIC SEQUENCE

When jazz musicians refer to "taking it out," they are essentially talking about using chromatic materials to create dissonance or obscure the harmony. There are countless ways to achieve this, but there are some conventional techniques that most players use. One of these techniques is **chromatic sequence**. A chromatic sequence is where a pattern, motive or melody is repeated by half step ascent or descent. The following examples illustrate how this device can be used over chord changes.

EXAMPLE 1

TRACK 35
0:00
CD 1

Often, these sequences are played over a pedal point in the bass.

EXAMPLE 2

When used in this manner, it creates tension and dissonance. One can use this technique in modal jazz, fusion, Latin, and other sub-genres.

EXAMPLE 3

Try your own chromatic sequences and let your imagination be your guide.

LESSON #36: TAKING IT OUT – SUPERIMPOSED HARMONIES

Another modern technique improvisers use to create dissonance in their solos is the concept of superimposing different harmonies over the standard chord. This practice was developed in the 1960s by players like Miles Davis, John Coltrane, McCoy Tyner, and Chick Corea. It was an attempt to bring fresh material into the lexicon of jazz vocabulary.

There are a variety of harmonies that can be superimposed, but some of the more common ones are playing lines transposed major or minor 2nds or 3rds above or below the chord. The lines will be diatonic in the new key. Pentatonic scales work particularly well in this application.

Play through the following examples.

MINOR 2nds

MAJOR 2nds

MAJOR AND MINOR 3rds

TRACK 36
0:21
CD 1

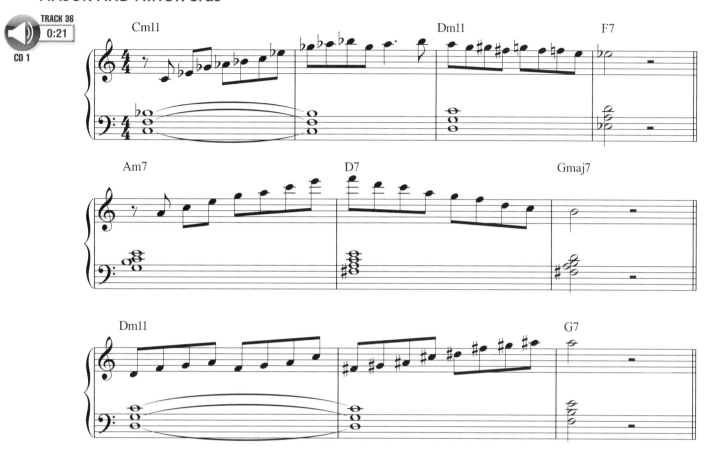

DIMINISHED 5ths

TRACK 36
0:38
CD 1

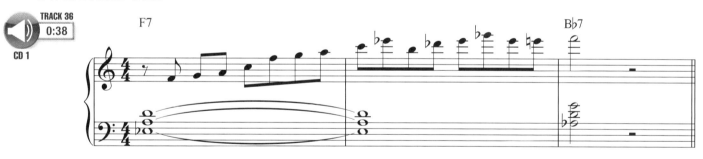

The farther the transposed key is from the original, the more dissonant it will sound. Experiment with your own ideas and let your own ear and sense of taste be your guide.

LESSON #37: THE ♯11 CHORD

Throughout history, musicians have had a love-hate relationship with the tritone. On one hand, it was the dissonant and vexing "devil's interval" that was forbidden in the writing of church organum. On the other hand, it contains the two tendency tones of our beloved V7 chord, and was later embraced by 20th century composers of the jazz, classical, and film music world as a valid and useful interval.

The ♯**11 chord** is interesting because it, in fact, contains not one tritone but two. There is a tritone between the 3rd and 7th, as with all dominant 7th chords, as well as a tritone between the root and the ♯11. Here are several ways to voice this chord in two hands.

EXAMPLE 1

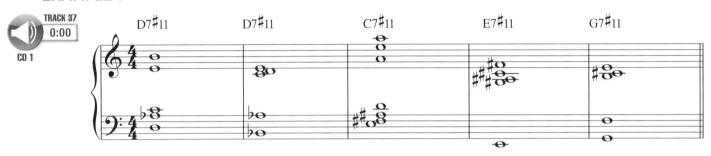

There are several scales that can be used to improvise over this chord. These scales are the diminished scale, the altered dominant scale, the whole tone scale, and the Lydian ♭7 scale.

EXAMPLE 2

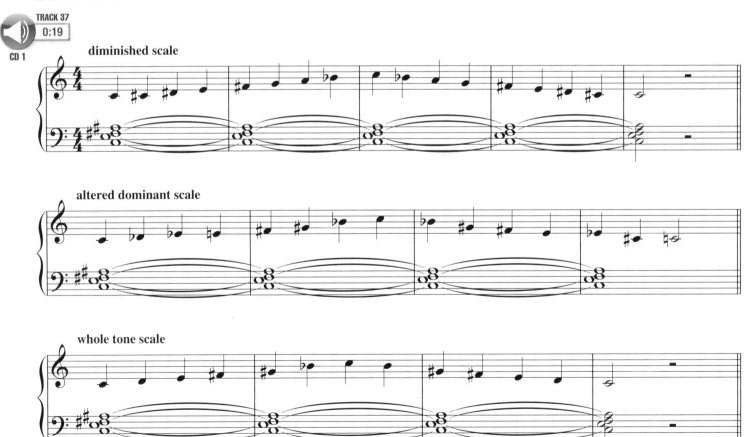

Play through the following improvised lines and choose your favorites. Learn them in all keys.

EXAMPLE 3

In tonal music, we have 12 equal-tempered notes at our disposal. However, even though they are equal in distance, they are most certainly not equal in importance or in function. When crafting satisfying bebop lines, the improviser must keep in mind the **hierarchy of notes** in order to place the more consonant ones on the harmonically strong beats of 1 and 3. At the top of the list are the chord tones of the **triad**, the strongest sounding and most satisfying notes of all.

EXAMPLE 1

Of these notes, the root is the most grounded, the 3rd firmly establishes the chord quality, and the 5th is somewhat less strong-sounding. Moving to the upper extensions of the chord there is the 7th, which is still strong, but less stable sounding than the triad notes.

EXAMPLE 2

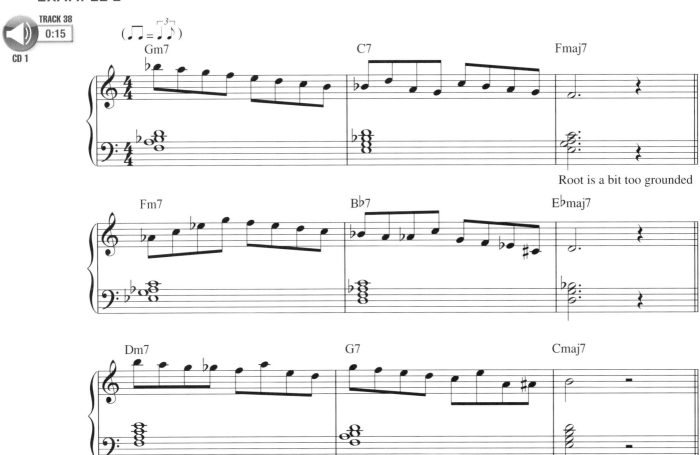

Root is a bit too grounded

The 9th and 13th are also reasonable notes to place on a harmonically strong beat. However, their result is much more colorful and less stable or consonant.

EXAMPLE 3

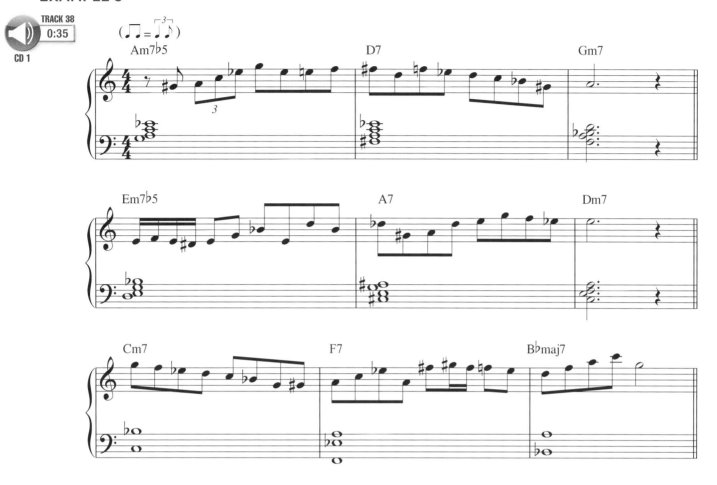

The 11th is generally the weakest diatonic note because of the instability of the 4th interval and its suspended quality.

EXAMPLE 4

Finally, the weakest and most unstable notes of all are the non-diatonic or chromatic tones. In bebop style, these notes should not be placed on a strong beat. Otherwise they should be resolved quickly, within an eighth note.

EXAMPLE 5

LESSON #39: 16TH-NOTE LINES

The construction and performance of **16th-note jazz lines** can be challenging. The velocity alone can make the task of playing through blazing-fast Parker, Powell, or Corea lines a daunting one. However, with the aid of your trusty metronome and some patience, these kinds of lines can indeed be mastered.

The first thing to consider is that the harmonic rhythm will be moving slower in relation to the speed of the notes. This means that you will play twice as many notes per chord as you would in eighth notes.

EXAMPLE 1

TRACK 39
0:00
CD 1

Because of this, you will have to remember that your chord tones still should fall on beats 1 and 3, even though your lines are moving twice as fast.

EXAMPLE 2

TRACK 39
0:10
CD 1

Try practicing the following 16th-note lines. Remember that in order to get faster at improvising these types of lines yourself, you must practice slowly at first, at a tempo in which you are able to improvise accurately. The tempo should be increased, incrementally, only when the previous tempo is mastered.

EXAMPLE 3

LESSON #40: THE WHOLE-TONE SCALE

The **whole-tone scale** is an unusual-sounding but handy scale for the improviser to have in their toolbox. The scale is not derived from the major scale, but from a succession of major 2nd intervals. As such, it is not considered tonal. It is a six-note scale and has a dissonant, unresolved feeling to it.

One interesting thing about it is that, no matter what note you start on, there are really only two whole-tone scales, a half step apart.

EXAMPLE 1

TRACK 40
0:00
CD 1

Another curious feature is that the scale contains six tritones, probably contributing to its unstable sound.

EXAMPLE 2

TRACK 40
0:17
CD 1

Also, the scale contains major 3rds, minor 6ths, and minor 7ths, so there are many chords that sound great under this scale, particularly altered dominant chords.

Try the following patterns based on the whole-tone scale.

EXAMPLE 3

TRACK 40
0:22
CD 1

The whole-tone scale can be used as part of a great melodic jazz phrase. Play through the following lines and pick your favorites to learn in 12 keys.

EXAMPLE 4

Try to come up with your own jazz lines incorporating the whole-tone scale.

LESSON #41: INTERPRETING A LEAD SHEET

I have noticed that students who are new to jazz tend to interpret **lead sheets** too literally. This makes sense when you consider that most pianists spend years playing music exactly as written prior to exploring jazz and improvisation. In this lesson, you will learn what is – and isn't – important when reading lead sheets.

Function of a Lead Sheet

Where sheet music of a classical piano sonata will show almost every aspect of a musical performance in exacting detail, a lead sheet can be thought of as a snapshot of one chorus of the tune. For this reason, it is important to understand that jazz pianists typically utilize any number of subtle variations of harmony, melody, and rhythm on any given chorus.

Stylizing Rhythm

The melodies of lead sheets are rarely intended to be played exactly as the rhythms are written. The reason for this lack of precision has to do with the fact that rhythms of standard tunes are usually stylized by the player to fit the tempo, groove, and context of the arrangement. (It should be pointed out that this is not unique to jazz: Baroque musicians embellished melodies with a similar amount of freedom in the time of J.S. Bach.) The following example shows the first phrase of "Autumn Leaves" as it is found in a fake book and a few of the many ways that the rhythms might be stylized:

EXAMPLE 1

Adding Color

As with rhythm, jazz pianists typically utilize a variety of chords on any given chorus of a tune. For example, where a lead sheet might indicate a simple major 6th chord, a jazz pianist might elect to use a major 7th, major 9th, major 6/9, or major 13th chord. In general, the 9th or 13th can be added to most major or major-minor 7th chords, and the 9th or 11th can be added to minor chords. Altered dominants may also be used in place of diatonic dominant 7th chords in some instances. (See Lesson 45 on altered chords and Lesson 46 on tritone substitution.) The following example shows a lead-sheet chord progression and the way it might be interpreted by a jazz pianist:

EXAMPLE 2

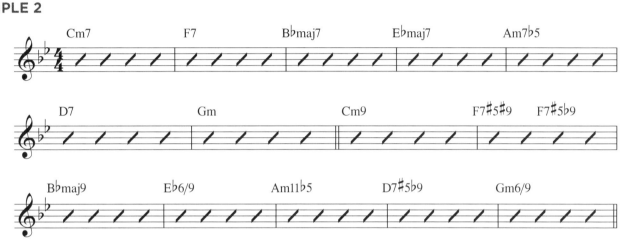

Primary Arrival Points

Most tunes consist of a number of primary key centers. In most cases, you will want to maintain these primary arrival points when you interpret a lead sheet. For example, the IV chord on the bridge of "Take the A Train" or the raised tonic on the bridge of "Body and Soul" are set in stone in this respect. In contrast, the chords that are used to set up the primary arrival points can usually be treated with a fair amount of freedom. The turnaround that is found in the last two bars of many tunes is one example of a progression of chords that can be adapted and altered in many ways. The pianist may elect to play the chords as is, play a variation such as those listed in the lesson on turnaround progressions, or simplify the progression by staying on a single chord or using just a ii-V-I. Similarly, the movement to the IV chord on the bridge of "Take the A Train" might be preceded by ii and V of the IV chord, just V of IV, or the pianist might move directly to the IV chord. The final example in this lesson illustrates one way to approach this decision-making process:

EXAMPLE 3

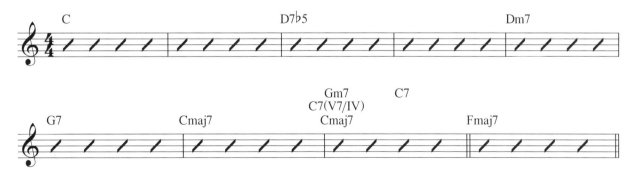

LESSON #42: ii-V-I VOICINGS: MAJOR/CLOSE POSITION

Two-five-one (ii-V-I) progressions are ubiquitous in jazz. Many standard tunes such as "Autumn Leaves," "Satin Doll," and "Honeysuckle Rose" are largely comprised of ii-V-I progressions in a variety of temporary key centers. Given that so many standard tunes feature ii-V-Is, it makes sense to practice these progressions so that you can sight read chord charts and learn songs more quickly. The voicings in this lesson can be played in the right hand over a bass line in the left hand, and they are also effective as a mid-range left-hand accompaniment for a solo.

Common Close-Position Voicings

One common close-position ii-V-I voicing can be seen in the following example. Notice how only one tone changes when moving from the ii to V chord (the 7th of the ii chord moves to the 3rd of the V chord).

EXAMPLE 1

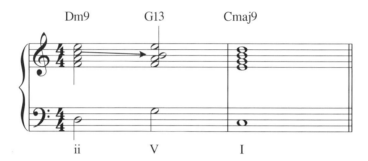

The following exercise is one of the most common "must know" voicings practiced by aspiring jazz pianists. Practice it as shown until the voicings are comfortable in both the left and right hand in all keys.

EXAMPLE 2

The previous exercise covers only six keys so be sure to start the exercise a half-step higher or lower to practice the other six keys:

EXAMPLE 3

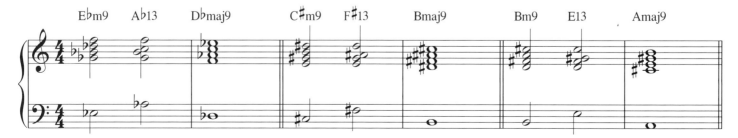

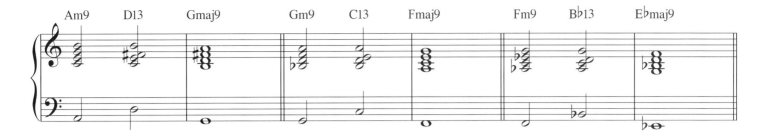

Another common close-position ii-V-I voicing utilizes a different starting inversion. In this case, the ii chord is built on the 7th of the chord (7-9-3-5). Practice the exercise as follows in both the right and left hand:

EXAMPLE 4

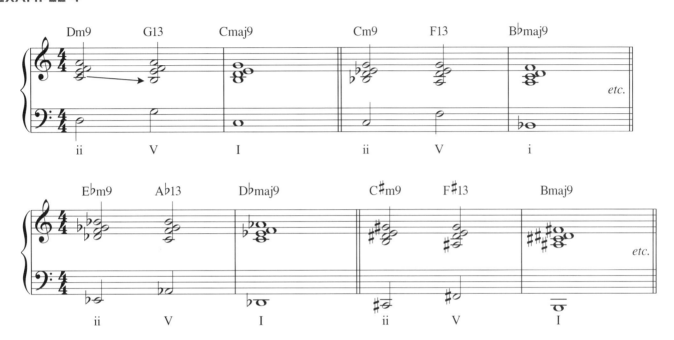

Once you are comfortable with both common versions of the ii-V-I progression you will be able to play through the chords of many jazz tunes with minimal movement between chords, something that is always a desirable aspect of voice leading. Here is one such example:

EXAMPLE 3

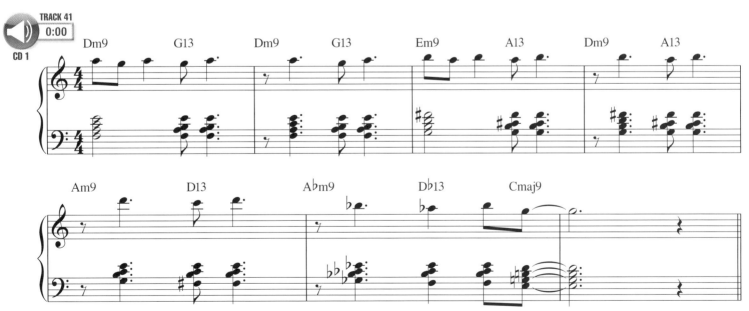

LESSON #43: ii-V-I VOICINGS: MINOR/CLOSE POSITION

Unlike ii-V-I voicings in a major key, the **ii chord in a minor ii-V-i progression** often sounds better without the 9th. The following ii-V-i progression will feel similar to the major ii-V-I voicings from the preceding lesson (e.g., the 7th of the ii chord resolves to the 3rd of the V chord), but a primary difference is that the ii chord is half-diminished. (An easy way to visualize a half-diminished chord is to think of a diminished triad with an interval of a minor 7th on top.) The chord is synonymous with a minor 7th with a diminished 5th. Also note that the lowered 5th (A♭ in the following example) is a common tone with the lowered 9th of the dominant. This is a common feature of ii-V-i progressions in a minor key.

EXAMPLE 1

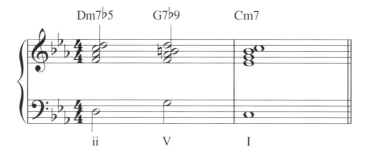

As with close-position voicings in a major key, practice the following exercises until you can fluently play ii-V-i voicings in any minor key. It is interesting to note that players use a variety of minor chords for the "arrival" i chord. The minor 6th chord shown in below has a slightly dark sound that works very well on tunes like "Autumn Leaves," but a minor 7th chord is also possible. Some players use a minor-major 7th chord which might be described as strident.

EXAMPLE 2

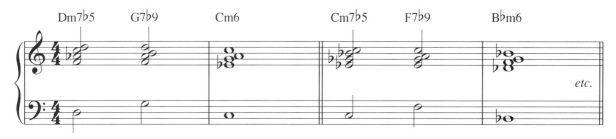

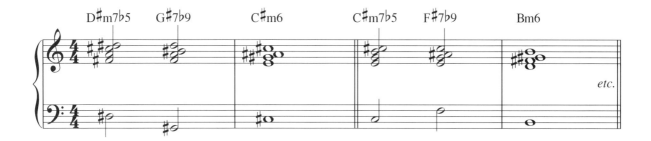

Another common inversion can be seen in the next example.

EXAMPLE 3

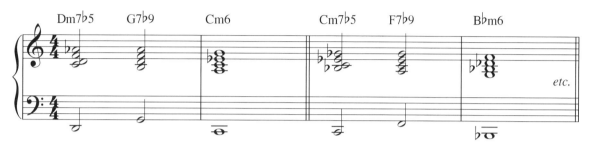

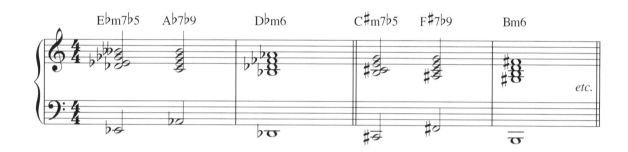

Remember that with the voicings shown in this chapter, there is always a chord inversion that is relatively close and can be utilized for smooth voice leading.

EXAMPLE 4

LESSON #44: DROP-2 VOICINGS

You may hear jazz musicians refer to **drop-2 voicings**. Drop-2 voicings are open voicings that can be very effective behind a solo or in the context of playing a jazz ballad. Where close position voicings can sound rich and meaty, drop-2 voicings might be described as subtly open.

Overview of Drop-2 Voicings

The theory behind drop-2 voicings is remarkably easy to visualize. Simply start with a good close-position voicing in any inversion and drop the second note from the top an octave, as in Example 1.

EXAMPLE 1

Given the open spacing between notes, drop-2 voicings are typically played with two notes in each hand or three notes in the right hand and one note in the left hand. The second approach is useful if you want to incorporate a bass note:

EXAMPLE 2

Two drop-2 inversions are particularly helpful. The chords below utilize the 3rd, 7th, 9th, and 5th of a given jazz chord:

EXAMPLE 3

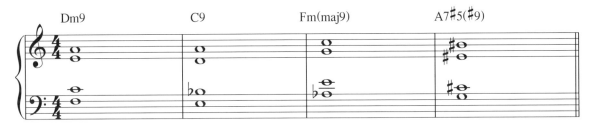

Notice how the notes 3-7-9-5 will tend to work for any chord type. Similarly, the inversion utilizing the 7th, 3rd, 5th, and 9th is also very common:

EXAMPLE 4

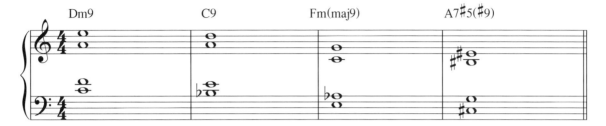

Practice the following ii-V-I voicings in all keys to develop fluency with many of the most common drop-2 voicings:

EXAMPLE 5

LESSON #45: ALTERED CHORDS

Some classical theorists describe **altered chords** as those in which the 5th has been altered, but I use a more liberal definition that includes chords in which the 5th and/or 9th have been altered. By far, the most common category of altered chords in jazz are altered dominant chords. In many instances, the 5th and 9th are altered, as in Example 1.

EXAMPLE 1

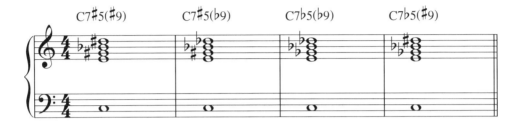

However, in some cases only the 5th is altered.

EXAMPLE 2

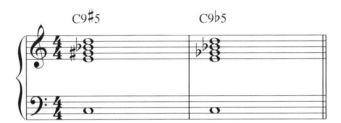

Similarly, the 9th may be altered but not the 5th:

EXAMPLE 3

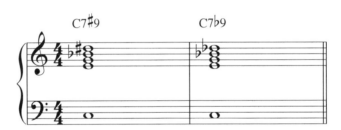

Function of Altered Chords

The most common reason for using altered chords is to strengthen the movement to a given tonic, or temporary tonic, chord. Such altered dominants, while not intrinsically better than unaltered chords, do have a stronger sense of motion toward the given arrival chord. Example 4 shows several common applications:

EXAMPLE 4

Utilizing Altered Chords

A good way to begin exploring the concept of altered chords is to experiment with alterations of the dominant or applied dominant chords. In general, altered chords will work if the altered tones don't conflict with the melody of the tune. Example 5 shows a diatonic (unaltered) progression and the application of several altered chords. Note how the alterations fit with the melody of the tune:

EXAMPLE 5

Practice Exercise

I have found that it is useful to practice altered dominants in the context of major and minor ii-V-I progressions. Play the diatonic ii-V-I below and explore a variety of altered 5ths and 9ths. You will find that, with a little practice, you will be able to incorporate altered chords on the fly.

EXAMPLE 6

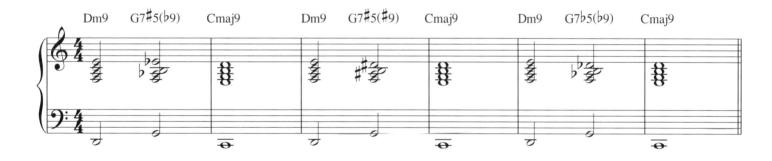

It is common for jazz musicians to modify the basic harmony of a standard tune, blues progression, or other improvisational vehicle, and the term **substitution** is sometimes used to describe the process of substituting or replacing chords in a "stock" progression. **Tritone substitution** represents a common category of harmonic substitutions that we will explore in this lesson.

Theory of Tritone Substitution

The tendency for a major-minor 7th chord (sometimes called a **dominant 7th**) to resolve down a 5th is very strong. You can test this by playing a G7 chord and resolving to C major and then to A minor. The deceptive resolution to A minor is startling and demonstrates the strength of the dominant-to-tonic relationship.

EXAMPLE 1

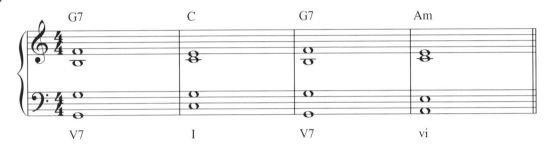

A tritone substitution takes advantage of the dominant/tonic relationship, but does so by utilizing a chromatic alteration. To understand how the process works, it is necessary to compare two major-minor 7th chords a tritone apart. Note how, in the next example, a G7 and D♭7 share the same 3rd and 7th (B, the 3rd of G7, is the 7th (C♭) of D♭7; F, the 7th of G7, is the 3rd of D♭7):

EXAMPLE 2

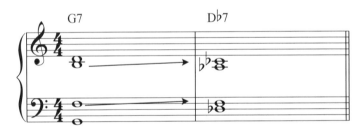

Tritone substitution takes advantage of the fact that the 3rd and 7th of a major-minor 7th chord are tendency tones that want to resolve to the root and 3rd of a tonic chord. The following three-note voicings demonstrate how the functional resolution of these tones is still fulfilled when the tritone is used:

EXAMPLE 3

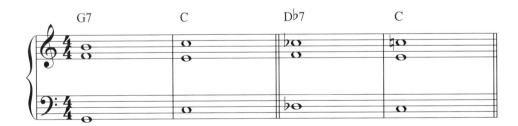

Using Tritone Substitution

In many cases, a major-minor 7th chord a tritone away can be substituted for a dominant 7th (e.g., G♭7 for C7, B7 for F7, or A♭7 for D7, and so on). Although the substitution is most frequently used for dominant 7ths, the technique may be applied to any major-minor 7th chord that moves down a 5th. For example, in a turnaround progression, secondary or applied dominants are sometimes used to strengthen the motion of descending 5ths (e.g., E7-A7-D7-G7). Tritone substitution can be used for some (or all) of the temporary dominants in Example 4.

EXAMPLE 4

LESSON #47: LINEAR CADENCE

A harmonic cadence is a temporary relaxation or cessation of harmonic activity. In this lesson we will explore the concept of a **linear cadence** – a type of cadence in which the independent movement of voices is emphasized.

Why Use Linear Motion?

A linear approach is one of the best antidotes against pedantic harmony. Linear motion can be a powerful technique and is associated with many of the greatest composers from J.S. Bach to Duke Ellington. It is characterized by a strong, but sometimes unexpected, sense of cadential motion. Example 1 demonstrates a linear approach to a basic ii-V-I progression:

EXAMPLE 1

Exploring Linear Motion

Although linear motion can be powerful, it can be a challenge to practice since the process can't be codified into a set of rules. However, there are certain tendencies that can provide context for exploration:

1. Treat each voice independently.

2. Be sensitive to tendency tones and their resolution.

3. Contrary motion is good.

4. Arrival chords are important.

One way to practice linear cadence is to use linear motion to connect the tones in a V7-I progression. Start by voicing the dominant and visualize the arrival voicing, as in Example 2.

EXAMPLE 2

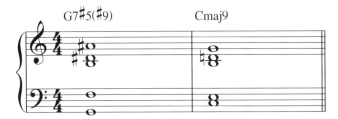

Next, explore independent motion for some or all of the notes in the dominant chord, and let some or all of the voices maintain independent movement toward the arrival chord. The following cadences demonstrate a few of the many options:

EXAMPLE 3

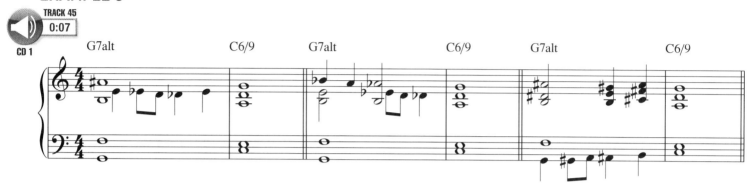

One of my favorite examples of linear cadence comes from an Oscar Peterson performance of "Little Girl Blue." Notice his masterful use of linear process in Example 4.

EXAMPLE 4

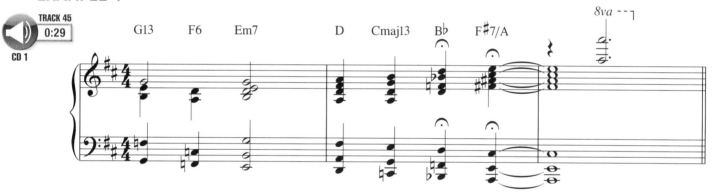

DIMINISHED 7TH CHORDS

Although diminished chords are not used as frequently as some other chord types in jazz, they can be very effective in some contexts. In this lesson, we will look at four useful applications.

Constructing a Diminished 7th Chord

Diminished 7th chords are easy to spell because they are symmetrical – each note in the chord is a minor 3rd above, or below, any other chord factor:

EXAMPLE 1

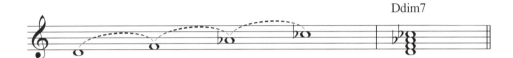

Adding Color

Although an unadorned diminished 7th can be effective, jazz musicians sometimes modify diminished chords to create a sound that might be described as "lush." One common approach is to add a note that is a whole step above one of the chord tones, as in Example 2:

EXAMPLE 2

Moving Between ii and iii

A common application of a diminished 7th chord is to connect the ii and iii chords in a progression. Notice how the technique works well for ascending and descending passages:

EXAMPLE 3

Tonicization

Another use of the diminished 7th chords is to tonicize a given arrival chord. For example, Bdim7 is the leading-tone diminished of C, so a Bdim7 can be used to tonicize any C chord, even if the C chord is not the tonic key. Although using a diminished 7th in this way can sound old-fashioned if the roots are placed in the bass register, the technique can be very effective when applied over the tonic:

EXAMPLE 4

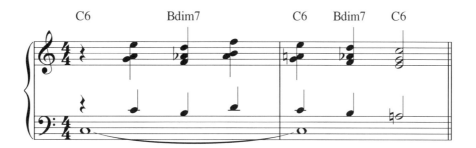

Embellishing Diminished

Another interesting application of diminished chords can be seen in the next example. In this application, a diminished 7th chord is used to embellish a major 7th chord that functions as the tonic in the key. (Classical theorists call these **embellishing diminished chords**). Notice how the 3rd and 5th of the diminished 7th resolve up to the same tones in the arrival chord. This technique provides a particularly compelling variation to the first bar of the standard tune "Misty."

EXAMPLE 5

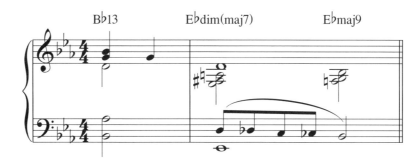

UTILIZING CHORD TONES IN AN IMPROVISATION

There are many ways to practice **improvisation**, such as using the melody of a tune, using scales, or applying motives, but a **deliberate use of chord tones** will provide a necessary foundation for nearly any tune. This lesson will focus on several concepts that will enable you to master this essential aspect of jazz musicianship.

Going Vertical

In order to master chord tones, it is necessary to become fluent in playing, and hearing the notes of common chord types. One useful exercise is to outline a given chord and each inversion, as in Example 1.

EXAMPLE 1

Be sure to explore other patterns. Many variations are possible, such as the patterns shown in Example 2.

EXAMPLE 2

Guide-Tone Lines

Chord tones arpeggiations can be useful to build a solo or to produce "sheets of sound," but the most useful application is to focus on chord tones for their melodic potential. One useful strategy is to practice what some jazz musicians refer to as guide-tone lines. My definition of a guide-tone line is a series of chord tones that effectively implies the underlying harmony. I have heard the tune "All the Things You Are" described as a perfect guide-tone line, and I think there is some truth in the statement. Let's look at the first phrase of the tune.

EXAMPLE 3

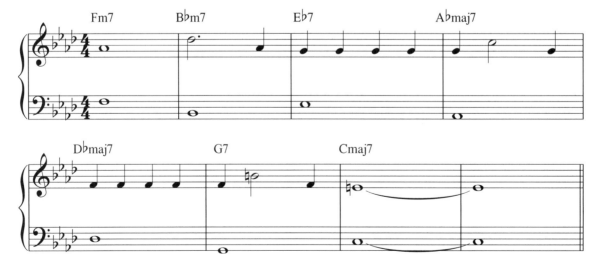

Notice how economically and effectively the harmony is implied in this standard tune. In fact, the melody and bass line are enough to clearly imply the progression. It is also interesting to note that the melody consists of a preponderance of 3rds and 7ths – the two chord tones that are most useful in implying a given chord type. Here is another guide tone over the same tune:

EXAMPLE 4

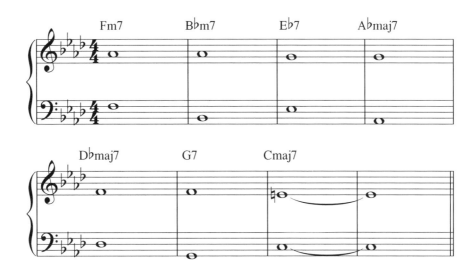

Applying Chord Tones to the Blues

A blues progression provides a useful vehicle for practicing chord tones. Experiment by using just one or two chord tones per chord and strive to make the chord tones melodic. Be sure to consider the tendency of a given chord tone as well as common ground between chord. For example, the 9th of the I chord is the 13th of the IV chord. Example 5 demonstrates one approach:

EXAMPLE 5

Although it can be a challenge to incorporate chord tones in a melodic way, with practice you will be able to effectively incorporate chord tones in your improvisations.

LESSON #50: NON-HARMONICS – NEIGHBOR TONES

Neighbor tones are a category of embellishing notes sometimes referred to as **non-harmonics**. I like to think of neighbor tones, and other non-harmonics such as changing tones and passing tones, as a sort of secret weapon for jazz improvisation. The concept is extremely simple, yet the results can be powerful.

What Is a Neighbor Tone?

As the name implies, a neighbor tone might be described as a tone that lives next door to a chord tone. For example, in a G major chord, the note C is an upper neighbor of the chord tone, B. Similarly, C is the lower neighbor to D, and E is the upper neighbor of D.

EXAMPLE 1

Note that, although the notes A and E are considered non-harmonics in the context of a G major triad, the notes are harmonic to G6/9 or Gmaj13.

Diatonic and Chromatic Neighbor Tones

Diatonic neighbor tones are neighbor tones that fit with a given key. In contrast, **chromatic neighbor tones** are outside of the given key. The most common chromatic neighbor tones are those that are a half-step below a given chord tone. For example, the A♯ and C♯ in Example 2 are examples of chromatic neighbor tones:

EXAMPLE 2

Practicing Neighbor Tones

One of the best ways to practice internalizing neighbor tones is to use neighbor tones to embellish all the notes of a given chord. Be sure to practice upper and lower neighbors as well as chromatic and diatonic versions:

EXAMPLE 3

Once you are comfortable playing neighbor tones on the fly, apply the concept to the chord changes of a blues or standard tune. Example 4 shows one such approach.

EXAMPLE 4

NON-HARMONICS – CHANGING TONES

Bop musicians such as Charlie Parker and Bud Powell were particularly adept at utilizing harmonic and non-harmonic tones in their improvisations. In my estimation, a key aspect of the bop language involves a fluent use of various non-harmonic tones. In a previous lesson you learned about neighbor tones, a common category of non-harmonic tones. In this lesson you will learn about a related concept known as **changing tones** or **double neighbor tones**.

What Are Changing Tones?

Changing tones are formed when upper and lower neighbor tones are combined. One way to visualize changing tones is to think about jumping on both sides of a given chord tone. Note that a common approach to playing changing tones is to use a whole step above and a half step below the given chord tone:

EXAMPLE 1

Practicing Changing Tones

As with passing tones, it is a good idea to practice applying changing tones to a single chord in order to develop fluency:

EXAMPLE 2

Using Other Chord Tones

Another common approach is to embellish a chord tone and then leap to another chord tone. Such embellishments are a common feature of many bop solos:

EXAMPLE 3

Applying Changing Tones to a Progression

One of the challenging aspects of utilizing changing tones is that the embellishment often happens before the arrival of a given chord. In order to develop an ear for the sound, practice applying changing tones to the root, 3rd, and 5th respectively.

EXAMPLE 4

The following lick demonstrates how changing tones can be useful in embellishing primary chord tones. With some practice, you will be able to effortlessly incorporate these useful non-harmonic tones.

EXAMPLE 5

NON-HARMONICS – PASSING TONES

In previous lessons, you learned about neighbor tones and changing tones, two important categories of non-harmonic tones. In this lesson, you will learn about **passing tones**, another important type of non-harmonic tones.

What Are Passing Tones?

Where neighbor tones and changing tones can be thought of as embellishments of a single chord tone, a passing tone can be thought of as a non-harmonic that connects two chord tones. For example, note how the note D connects the chord tones C and E in the next illustration:

EXAMPLE 1

Similarly, the note F can be used to pass between E and G:

EXAMPLE 2

Chromatic and Diatonic Passing Tones

The preceding examples are **diatonic passing tones**. That is, they are non-harmonics that are diatonic to the key. **Chromatic passing tones** can also be very effective. Notice how diatonic and chromatic passing tones are combined to form an effective line in the next example:

EXAMPLE 3

Practicing Passing Tones

In my estimation, scale fragments provide the best vehicle for learning to internalize passing tones. For example, the so-called **bop scale** utilizes both chromatic and diatonic passing tones over a V or ii-V progression:

EXAMPLE 4

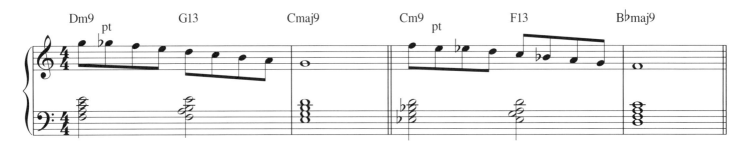

Similarly, a scale pattern like Example 5 can be applied to a circle progression in order to develop fluency:

EXAMPLE 5

Applying Passing Tones to a Progression

Once you have learned to apply passing tones to a given chord or circle progression, it will be relatively easy to apply the concept to a progression of chords. As with changing tones, try to think ahead when using passing tones to connect chord tones in a harmonic progression.

EXAMPLE 6

MELODIC MINOR SCALES – FOUR APPLICATIONS

In this lesson, you will learn to apply **melodic minor scales** to four different chord types. The concept will open the door to many of the sounds associated with modern jazz pianists.

Visualizing a Melodic Minor Scale

In jazz, the ascending form of the melodic minor scale is almost always used, regardless of the direction of the line. One easy way to visualize the scale is to think of a major scale with a minor 3rd. For example, play the white-note C major scale and replace the major 3rd (E) with a minor 3rd (E♭) to form a melodic minor scale:

EXAMPLE 1

Tipping a Chord on Its Side

Some of the applications of melodic minor scales in this lesson may seem counterintuitive, so it is helpful to remember that a scale can usually be thought of as a chord that has been tipped on its side. Notice how, in the next example, a C melodic minor scale is formed by making a scale from all of the notes of a C min(maj13) chord:

EXAMPLE 2

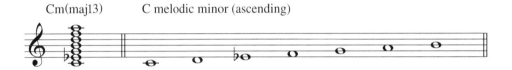

Application 1: Tonic Minor

The preceding example leads us to a first application: Use a melodic minor scale based on the root of the chord for any minor 6, minor 6/9, minor(maj7), minor(maj9) or similar chord.

EXAMPLE 3

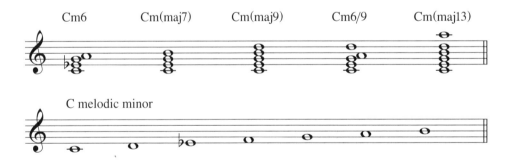

Application 2: Half-diminished

Melodic minor scales can also be applied to **half-diminished chords**. Simply construct a melodic minor starting on the 3rd of the chord. In the next example, a C melodic minor provides all of the chord tones including common extensions for an Amin7♭5.

EXAMPLE 4

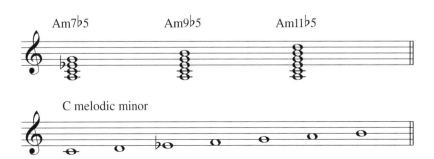

Application 3: Altered

An **altered scale** is formed by playing a melodic minor scale up one half step from the root of an altered dominant chord. Although this scale seems particularly unintuitive, the resulting scale consists of the root, 3rd, 7th, as well as altered 5ths and 9ths:

EXAMPLE 5

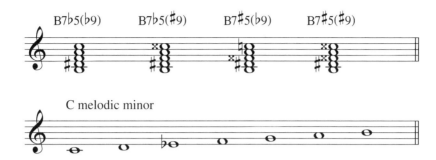

Application 4: Lydian Dominant

Melodic minor scales can also be applied to so-called **Lydian dominant chords**. Simply construct a melodic minor scale starting on the 5th of the chord. In this case, the scale provides the root, 3rd, and 7th as well as extensions including the 9th, raised 11th, and 13th:

EXAMPLE 6

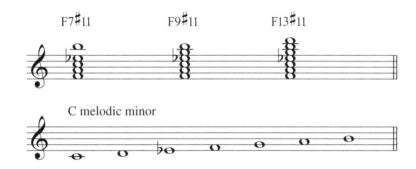

Practicing Applications of Melodic Minor Scales

A minor ii-V-i progression provides a perfect vehicle for practicing melodic minor scales since three (or four) of the scales can be applied to the progression:

EXAMPLE 7

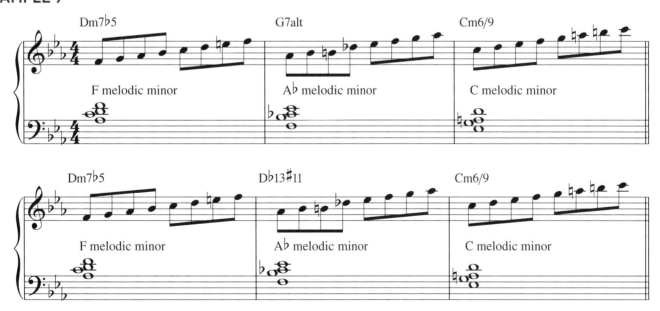

LESSON #54: SCALE-TONE TRIADS & 7TH CHORDS

In this lesson, you will learn how to explore the melodic potential of triads and 7th chords that are found within a scale. The technique has a virtually limitless potential for interesting melodies and patterns, and the concept is often heard in the improvisations of Bill Evans, Herbie Hancock, and other musicians associated with modern jazz.

Basic Concept

Some jazz musicians use the term **scale-tone triad** or **scale-tone 7th** to describe an approach to utilizing the triads and 7th chords that are found within a given scale. In the key of C, it is easy to observe that the scale contains seven triads:

EXAMPLE 1

Similarly, a number of 7th chords can also be found:

EXAMPLE 2

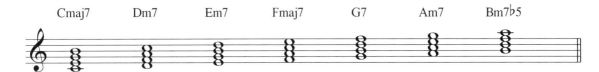

This concept has profound melodic implications. For example, notice how an Fmaj7, Em7, Dm7, and Cmaj7 are implied over a Dm11 chord in the next example. (Note that a D Dorian scale contains the same notes as C major.)

EXAMPLE 3

As you can hear in Example 3, the individual 7th chords found in a D Dorian scale have a rich melodic potential, but the scale-tone chords also work together to imply the underlying modality.

Applying Scale-Tone Concepts to an Altered Scale

The concept can be applied to most scales and modes including the altered scale. The triads found in C melodic minor, the altered scale for B7alt, are shown below. Note the order of triads in a melodic minor scale: minor, minor, augmented, major, major, diminished, diminished. This will be useful when you practice playing triads over altered chords and other advanced harmonies.

EXAMPLE 4

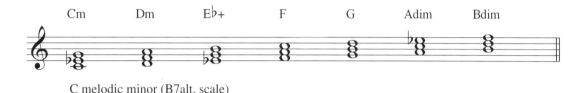

C melodic minor (B7alt. scale)

Example 5 shows how scale-tone triads might be utilized over a minor ii-V-i progression. A different application of a melodic minor scale is used over each chord change.

EXAMPLE 5

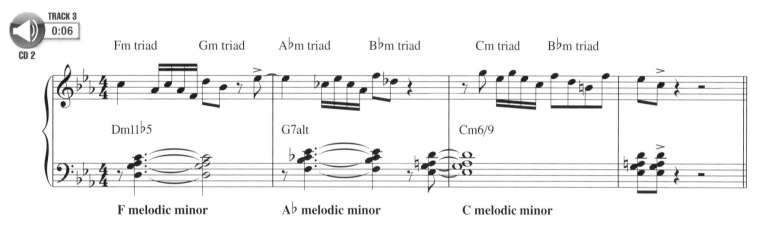

Although scale-tone triads can be difficult to master, diligent practice will yield huge dividends in being able to utilize the vast melodic potential of these structures. You may also find that thinking of triads in this way can simplify a set of changes that might ordinarily seem very challenging.

LESSON #55: MELODIC SETS

Music theorists sometimes organize a series of pitches into a collection known as a **set**. Although a discussion of set theory is beyond the scope of this book, the idea of visualizing a motive as a **melodic set** can be a powerful improvisational device. I once heard a lecture recital by New York saxophonist John O'Gallagher, a player who has internalized the concept as it relates to 12-tone theory to a very high level, and was very impressed by his melodic inventiveness. In this lesson, we will explore a number of concepts that will help you incorporate melodic sets into your playing.

Creating a Melodic Set

One way to visualize a melodic set is to think of a melodic shape. The shape might consist of a step and a leap, two steps, two steps and a leap, or some other form. The following shape consists of a step and jump of a 3rd, and the notes come from the G Dorian scale, a scale that works well for the given chord, Gm7:

EXAMPLE 1

Permutations

The set or shape can be manipulated in any number of ways, such as reordering or transposing notes, or playing the tones as a chord – or **verticalization**, as it is known in set theory parlance. Example 2 illustrates several permutations.

EXAMPLE 2

These simple permutations can yield an improvisation that maintains an organic quality, due in large part to the unifying influence of the underlying set:

EXAMPLE 3

Applying a Set to a Set of Chord Changes

Sets can be an incredibly powerful improvisational resource. In the next example, the set G-A-C is applied to a progression of chords. One way to apply the set in this context is to visualize the set as a series of intervals. For example, a classical theorist would place the pitches in ascending order so that the bounding interval is the smallest possible interval. The pitches are then numbered according to the number of half steps from the first interval. The first note is labeled zero:

EXAMPLE 4

This abstraction makes it easy to apply the set to any chord/scale relationship. Of course it is not necessary to use the traditional numbering system. It may be advantageous simply to visualize the preceding set as a whole step and minor 3rd.

The strength of this approach becomes evident when the set is applied to a variety of scales, as in the Example 5:

EXAMPLE 5

LESSON #56: RHYTHM STREAMS

I have heard jazz musicians describe rhythm as a series of streams. The streams are characterized by a specific division, subdivision, or rhythmic feel, and the improviser can step freely from one stream to another. In this lesson, you will expand your rhythmic palette by learning how to visualize and practice **rhythm streams**. The concept can help you internalize a high level of rhythmic fluency that is characteristic of Bill Evans and other modern jazz pianists.

Practicing Rhythm Streams

The best way to practice rhythm streams is to improvise solely within the given stream until it becomes second nature. The following examples demonstrate some of the most common rhythm streams heard in jazz: swing eighths, double-time 16ths, quarter-note triplet, and triplet-eighths.

EXAMPLES 1–4

Combining Streams

The real power of visualizing rhythm in this way comes from being able to combine the rhythms on the fly. One way to develop fluency is to deliberately incorporate the rhythm streams in a practice etude. The next etude demonstrates how the streams could be combined into groupings of two beats:

EXAMPLE 5

In my estimation, the best way to incorporate these concepts in an organic way is to let the motivic elements of a solo determine the use of rhythm streams. Like many aspects of improvisation, such streams will likely not appear without deliberate practice, but they can appear in an organic way once the concepts have been thoroughly internalized. The following example from a Bill Evans transcription demonstrates a masterful use of rhythm:

EXAMPLE 6

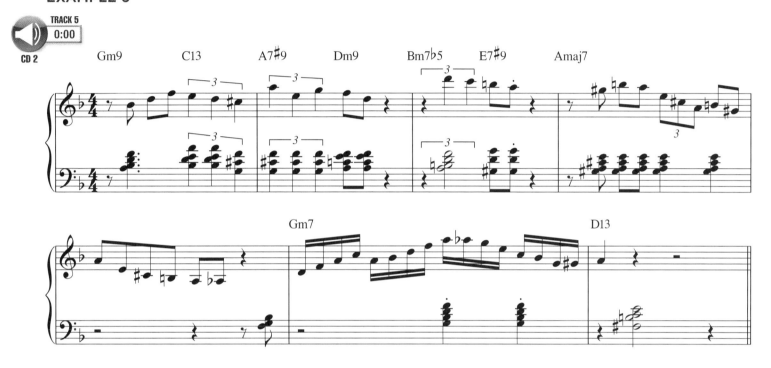

LESSON #57: MOTIVIC ETUDES

The word **lick** has a negative connotation in jazz. So-called "lick players" are derided for plugging in pat phrases in a predictable way. However, what many younger players don't realize is that incorporating licks can be an important step in internalizing the language of jazz. A language analogy may be helpful in illustrating the point: Children learn to speak a language by mimicking a few simple words such as mom, dad, yes, no, and so on. Relating this concept to jazz, such words might be thought of as building-block "licks." The child uses the words without a sense of context or nuance. Over time, the child internalizes a larger vocabulary and begins to combine the words in new ways with increasing subtlety and sophistication. In a similar way, a mature jazz musician will understand the language of jazz, but will avoid using the words or "licks" of the language in a pedantic fashion.

Practice Etudes

There is no getting around the fact that, in order to be fluent in jazz, it is necessary to internalize the language of jazz and develop fluency on the instrument. This is where the concept of **motivic etudes** really shines. One of the best ways to develop such fluency is to practice motives in all keys. Although practicing motives around the Circle of 5ths is always a good idea, be sure to vary the order of keys such as playing ascending half-steps, major 3rds, or some other pattern. The following examples demonstrate several strategies for internalizing the primary motive from "Honeysuckle Rose," a common jazz motive:

Adapting a Motive

Once you have internalized a motive in all keys, take the time to consider other ways in which the motive might be applied. For example, the "Honeysuckle Rose" motive could be applied to any number of chords in addition to a simple ii-V progression:

Modifying a Motive

It is also essential to practice motivic permutations. Consider changing the order of notes, altering the rhythm, embellishing the notes, leaving notes out, altering the intervals to fit a different harmonic context, or any number of other permutations. Such practice will move you out of the realm of "lick player" into the realm of "organic player" in much the same way that a master of prose can utilize ordinary words in an artistic way.

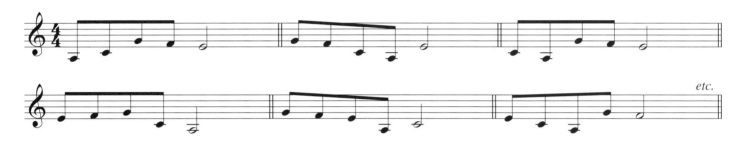

The following example demonstrates how a simple idea such as the "Honeysuckle Rose" motive could be transformed into an effective seed for a solo.

LESSON #58: SCALE-TONE VOICING

In this lesson, you will learn to explore and incorporate **scale-tone harmony**, a concept that can provide new insights into voicing what might otherwise be an ordinary progression of chords.

What Are Scale-Tone Chords?

Each major scale, minor scale, and mode contains a series of triads. In the key of C major, for example, it is easy to see that the scale is comprised of triads in the order of: major, minor, minor, major, major, minor, diminished:

EXAMPLE 1

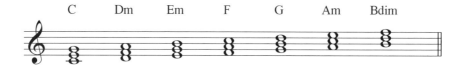

Instead of voicing chords in 3rds over a root, scale-tone triads can be used to imply the sound of a given harmony or mode without necessarily using tertian building blocks. Likely the most famous example of scale-tone voicing can be heard in "So What," a tune on Miles Davis's seminal *Kind of Blue* recording. In this example, the underlying Dm11 chord and D Dorian mode are clearly evident, but the harmonies primarily come from the mode, not from a vertical construction:

EXAMPLE 2

Using Scale-Tone Chords in Modal Jazz

The preceding approach works well for most modal progressions. Although quartal voicings (chords built in 4ths) can be particularly effective, tertian voicings can also sound great. The next example demonstrates both approaches as applied to an Fmaj7#11 chord. Notice how the scale-tone triads are not in root position. In my experience, first and second inversion triads are almost always more effective that root-position triads when voicing scale-tone harmonies.

EXAMPLE 3

Using Scale-Tone Chords in Blues

Scale-tone triads can also be effective in the context of blues and related genres. For example, the first-inversion triads found in a G Mixolydian scale are shown below and then applied to a G7 vamp in Example 5.

EXAMPLE 4

EXAMPLE 5

Using Scale-Tone Chords in Standard Tunes

As long as you are fluent with the common chord/scale relationships, it will be possible to apply the concept of scale-tone triads to standard tunes. Although this approach can be difficult to master, it can yield some interesting insights into traditional progressions. Example 6 demonstrates how the concept could be applied to a common progression of chords. A dashed line indicates the various scales from which the triads were constructed.

EXAMPLE 6

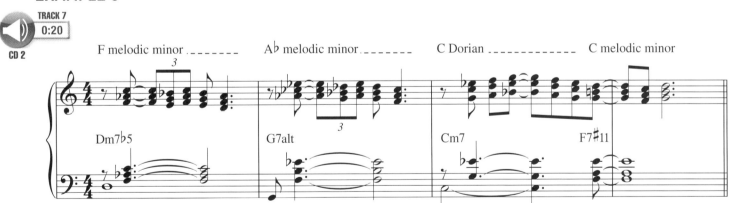

SIMPLIFYING EXTENSIONS WITH POLYCHORDS

One of the most challenging aspects of harmony for a budding jazz pianist is learning to play chords on the fly. There is a lot to think about, including the notes of the chords, possible extensions and alterations, and the actual voicing to be used. In some cases, visualizing common voicings as a **polychord** can simplify the process.

Simplifying Altered Voicings

Many altered voicings can be visualized as a simple triad over a 3rd and 7th (or root, 3rd, and 7th) in the left hand. Several common variants are shown below:

EXAMPLE 1

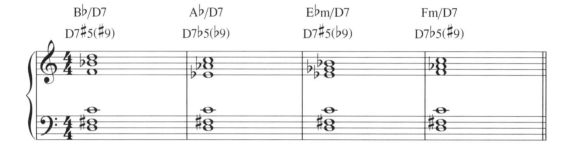

Thinking of voicings in this way will help you to play the voicing in other keys. For example, it is relatively easy to visualize a triad a major 6th above a given root, and that triad can be used to easily voice a dominant 13th chord with a lowered 9th in any key:

EXAMPLE 2

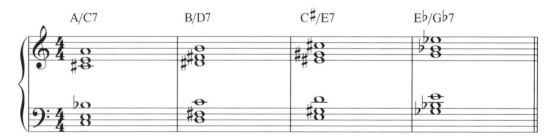

Lydian Chords

One of the most common polychord voicings of all is used to imply a Lydian or the so-called **Lydian dominant**, as in Example 3. Note that the triad is simply a whole-step above the root:

EXAMPLE 3

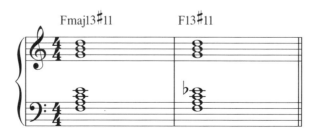

Major Chords

The concept can also be applied to more traditional chords, as in Example 4. The key is to visualize a simple triad in the right hand over a building block structure in the left:

EXAMPLE 4

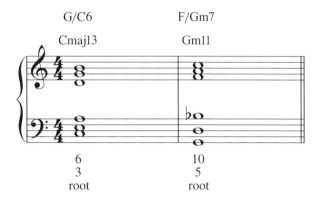

Minor Chords

The "So What" voicing from the lesson on scale-tone triads (Lesson 54) can also be visualized as a sort of polychord. In fact, all of the "trick" voicings in this lesson can be explored in more depth by applying the concept of scale-tone triads to voicing. The difference is that visualizing voicings as polychords may make it easier to play the structures in other keys.

EXAMPLE 5

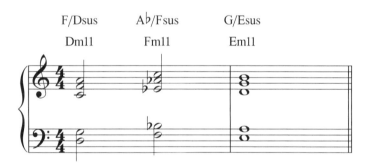

Other lessons are devoted to the theory and practice of drop-2 voicings, a category of chords very useful in jazz. In this lesson, you will learn how to utilize diminished 7th chords to tonicize drop-2 voicings. I first learned of the technique from jazz great Bill Dobbins, a professor at the Eastman School of Music.

Tonicization

A dominant 7th chord or leading-tone diminished can be used to temporarily tonicize a given arrival chord. For example, a Bdim or G7 can be used to tonicize a C chord, and F#dim or D7 tonicizes a G major chord. Tonicization can be a particularly effective technique in the context of drop-2 voicings. In Example 1, notice how Bdim provides a useful connection between two inversions of C6.

EXAMPLE 1

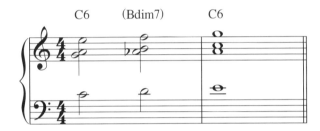

The technique is similarly effective in minor keys. Note the evocative sound of the following excerpt:

EXAMPLE 2

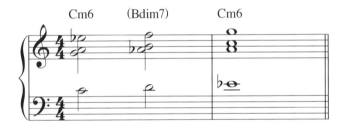

Tonicizing an Upper Structure

Interestingly, tonicization can be applied to just the upper structure of a voicing. Although Example 2 works well for a Cm6, the same notes can imply an F9. Notice how Bdim tonicizes Cm6, the upper structure of F9 in the following example. Although this concept might seem overly abstract, the important thing to remember is that the tonicizing chord can be applied to either the root of the chord or the "root" of any recognizable structure within the chord:

EXAMPLE 3

TRACK 8
0:00

CD 2

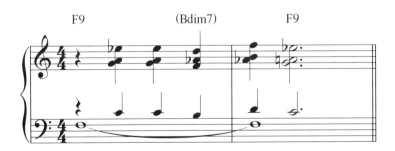

I particularly like to use this sound when comping on a blues. Play through Example 4 to get a feel for the concept.

EXAMPLE 4

TRACK 8
0:05
CD 2

Practice Etudes

One useful exercise, suggested by Professor Dobbins, is to alternate inversions of a major 6 drop-2 (or close-position voicing) with a tonicizing diminished chord. Practice playing up and down the scale and add the extra A♭ passing tone as shown in Example 5.

EXAMPLE 5

A similar exercise can be applied to minor 6th chords:

EXAMPLE 6

LESSON #61: PENTATONIC SCALES

Some modern jazz musicians utilize **pentatonic scales**. The scales are useful because a single pentatonic can be applied to many chords, and pentatonic scales tend to evoke a modern/modal mood that can be effective in many contexts.

Practicing Pentatonic Scales

One of the best ways to practice a pentatonic scale is to play ascending and descending patterns in order to develop digital and aural fluency.

EXAMPLES 1–2

Repeating-note patterns can also be useful. There is any number of variations, such as the following:

EXAMPLES 3–4

Applying Pentatonic Scales

One of the great things about pentatonic scales is that a single scale can be used for many different chords. One way to visualize this relationship is to think about chords that come from the key of the pentatonic. For example, a C major pentatonic could be used for the following chords. (Note that there are also several applications to chords in other keys such as B♭maj7♯11.)

EXAMPLE 5

Example 6 demonstrates one way that pentatonics could be applied to a progression of chords:

EXAMPLE 6

TRACK 9
0:00
CD 2

INTRODUCTION TO THE BLUES

Most jazz players have at least a modicum of blues in their playing, and blues is an essential ingredient of many jazz genres. It could even be said that blues is at the core of jazz itself. This lesson will focus on blues fundamentals.

Defining Blues

There are several ways to define the term **blues**. Blues can refer to a state of mind, as in "I have the blues." Blues can also refer to a style of playing. For example, players like Gene Harris and Oscar Peterson utilized lots of blues elements in their playing. The term can also refer to a progression of chords, usually the 12-bar blues.

Call and Response

Some musicians use the term **call and response** to refer to the question-and-answer phrasing that is often evident in blues. Using letters to indicate this phrasing, the blues form could be represented by the letters AAB. The concept is particularly clear when you relate the form to blues lyrics such as Bessie Smith's performance of "Lost Your Head Blues."

A: I was with you, baby, when you didn't have a dime.

A: I was with you, baby, when you didn't have a dime.

B: Now since you've got plenty of money, you have thrown your good gal down.

A 12-bar blues, the most common blues form, represents a harmonic version of the AAB call-and-response form. Although there are many variations of the basic blues progression, the following form is common:

EXAMPLE 1

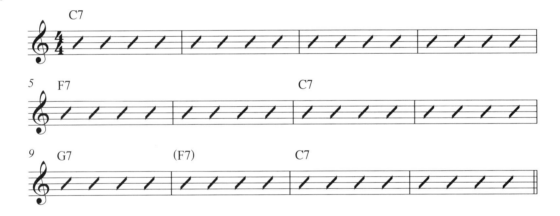

Riffs

Riffs are repeating phrases, usually two or four bars, that are an essential element of some forms of blues expression. The best riffs tend to be those that are simple. For example, "C-Jam Blues," also known as "Duke's Place," is a well-known tune based on a riff. Repeat the following riff over the previous 12-bar progression to hear how the riff works against the changes:

EXAMPLE 2

As with call and response, some players alter the third iteration of a four-bar riff to create the call-and-response effect.

Blues Scales

Although it is rare to hear a jazz musician use a verbatim version of the **blues scale**, the scale does provide a palette of notes frequently used in blues. To explore the sound of the scale, improvise with the blues scale in the right hand over the basic blues progression shown in Example 1.

EXAMPLE 3

Other Good Notes

Many excellent riffs and blues licks come from what I like to call the "other good notes." These tones, (sol, la, do, and re in a major key), fit nicely with all of the chords in a blues progression and can provide a great starting point in developing lines that are melodic.

EXAMPLE 4

Using Chord Tones

Chord tones can also be a useful resource when improvising on the blues. In fact, early jazz musicians such as Louis Armstrong and Sidney Bechet had a sophisticated harmonic sense, so the use of chord tones in blues improvisation goes back to the roots of the genre. The next excerpt illustrates how chord tones might be utilized in a blues performance. Note how the major 3rd of the tonic chord is a used in this illustration even though the note is not found in the blues scale:

EXAMPLE 5

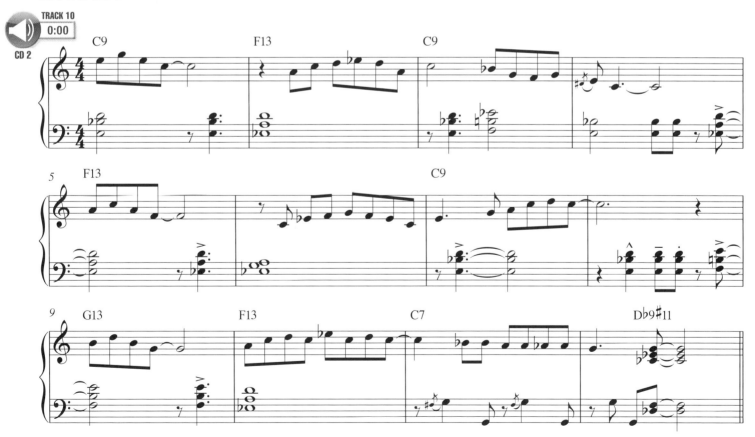

Blues is at the core of jazz, and most players use at least some blues vocabulary in their playing. This lesson will focus on some of the blues vocabulary that is associated with jazz piano.

Blue Notes

Where jazz vocalists, wind, and brass players can incorporate true **blue notes** – notes that are purposely out of tune – jazz pianists can only create the illusion of a blue note. In most cases, one or two grace notes can be used to create the effect of a blue note:

EXAMPLE 1

Pedal Point

In many cases, a **pedal point** can be combined with grace notes to accentuate the effect of blue notes in a passage. Notice how a repeating C is used over a fragment of the blues scale:

EXAMPLE 2

The repeating pedal tone can also be placed under a blues motive.

EXAMPLE 3

Scale-Tone 3rds

Scale-tone 3rds are frequently used by pianists such as Oscar Peterson and Gene Harris, two of the many jazz pianists that utilize blues elements in their playing. Experiment by placing scale-tone 3rds over a repeating pedal:

EXAMPLE 4

Repeating Patterns

Repeating patterns can be incorporated to help create a sense of blues style and inflection. Here are a few of my favorites:

EXAMPLE 5

Cross Rhythm

Repeating patterns can also be used to establish a **cross rhythm**, a rhythm that is at odds with the prevailing rhythm. Cross rhythms are frequently heard in blues solos and can be particularly effective at the climax of a solo:

EXAMPLE 6

Practical Application

The following solo excerpt, which was transcribed from an Oscar Peterson recording, demonstrates a number of the concepts described in this lesson:

EXAMPLE 7

LESSON #64: BEBOP BLUES

Most players are familiar with at least a few forms of the 12-bar blues. In this lesson you will learn to apply additional harmonies to the 12-bar blues in a way that is characteristic of many bebop tunes.

Basic Blues

Note the primary arrival points of the following basic 12-bar blues progression. Although there are many variations, most of the arrival points remain, even though many additional chords may be utilized:

EXAMPLE 1

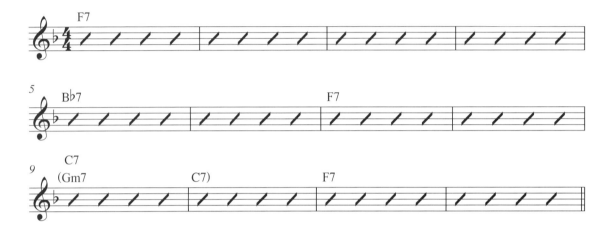

Tonicization

The concept of **tonicization**, using an applied major-minor 7th to strengthen the movement to a temporary tonic, can be implemented effectively in the progression. Note how a ii and V of the IV chord are used in the bar 4, and ii and V of the ii chord create a strong sense of movement to the last line of the progression.

EXAMPLE 2

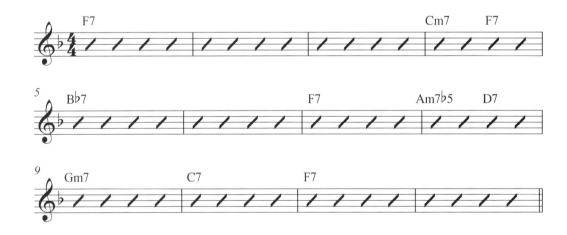

Tonicizing chord groups can also be effective in the first line. In the next example, a circle progression of temporary ii-V-I progressions creates an interesting sense of movement to the IV chord in the second line.

EXAMPLE 3

In Example 4, temporary ii-V-Is are used throughout the progression. Although this variation is very different from a simple 12-bar blues, all of the primary arrival chords are still evident in the progression. This progression is sometimes referred to as "Bird Blues" and comes from "Blues for Alice," a popular bebop tune that utilizes many re-harmonizations of the basic blues form.

EXAMPLE 4

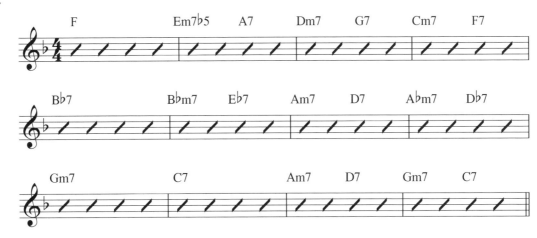

WALKING BASS LINES

Although **walking bass lines** are infrequently used by jazz pianists, notable players including Oscar Peterson and Billy Taylor use them on occasion. In addition to being useful in performance, walking bass lines are an invaluable technique to accompany improvisation students or as an accompaniment to your own melodic explorations.

Practicing Bass Lines

It can be tricky to develop the independence to play an effective bass line while soloing or comping in the right hand, but rest assured that it is not unduly difficult with some practice. My best advice is to practice the following etudes until you can apply each concept to any set of changes and let the left hand fly on autopilot. As the sounds become second nature, you will be able to play lines that are more sophisticated by relying on these foundational concepts.

Chord Tones

The primary function of a bass line is to imply the chords and provide a rhythmic anchor. A good starting place is to play roots and 5ths in a two-feel, as in Example 1.

EXAMPLE 1

Four on the Floor

A next step is to repeat notes to make four beats per measure. At this point, simply repeat the root as necessary to fill in all four beats. Experiment by adding an occasional 3rd, as in Example 2.

EXAMPLE 2

Passing Tones

Passing tones provide a nice way to connect the primary chord tones of a bass line. Notice how an occasional passing tone provides a more graceful contour in the following line:

EXAMPLE 3

Chromatic Approach

A useful fourth step is to explore chromatic approach tones on beat 4 of any measure preceding a chord change. Although most bass players would avoid playing as many approach tones as in the next example, the etude will help you develop fluency.

EXAMPLE 4

Eighth Notes and Triplets

An occasional eighth-note grouping or a triplet can provide a wonderful sense of movement and style to a bass line. In order to practice the technique, try adding two eighth notes or a triplet-eighth arpeggio every four bars or so until the technique is comfortable. (You will probably want to avoid using so many embellishments when playing bass lines in public.)

EXAMPLE 5

TRACK 12
0:00
CD 2

Practical Application

The following bass line demonstrates how the concepts in this lesson could be applied to the construction of an effective bass line. I would stress that it will be possible to create similar bass lines in real time once you have mastered each of the building block examples presented in this lesson.

EXAMPLE 6

TRACK 12
0:20
CD 2

LESSON #66: LOCKED HANDS

The concept of **locked-hands voicing** is often associated with the pianist Milt Buckner, and the technique was used by George Shearing, Nat Cole, Oscar Peterson, and many other jazz pianists. The name comes from the fact that both hands are placed in close proximity and appear to be locked together.

Locked-Hands Voicings

The most common locked-hands voicing is characterized by a close-position voicing in the right hand. The key to successful locked-hands voicing is to create a four-note right-hand voicing that sounds rich and has an appropriate amount of color. In general, a four-note voicing consisting of any inversion of the 3rd, 5th, 7th, and 9th will work. In some cases, the 13th can replace the 5th, and altered 5ths and 9ths are sometimes used on dominant chords. To complete the locked-hands voicing, simply double the top note of the right-hand voicing an octave lower in the left hand, as in the following illustration:

EXAMPLE 1

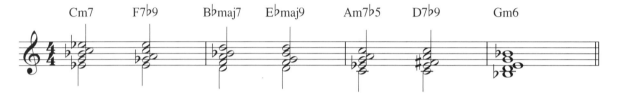

Another version of locked hands can be constructed by creating a drop-2 voicing and doubling the top note an octave lower. This technique is sometimes referred to as **thickened-line voicing**:

EXAMPLE 2

Practicing Locked Hands: Inversions

In general, the best way to practice locked-hands voicings is to become fluent with right-hand inversions of common chord types. For example, use a variety of major 6th and major 9th inversions to harmonize a pentatonic melody, as in Example 3. Similar exercises can be played for other chord types, including minor 9th and dominant 9th chords.

EXAMPLE 3

Non-harmonic Solutions

Most melodies contain non-harmonics, notes that don't "fit" a given chord. There are several non-harmonic solutions that can be used to harmonize non-harmonic tones, including tonicization, planing, and shifting.

To **tonicize**, simply use the leading-tone diminished or dominant of the given chord:

EXAMPLE 4

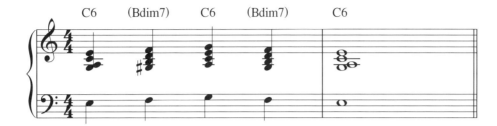

In many cases, **diatonic planing** can be used to handle non-harmonic tones. Visualize a starting voicing and arrival chord and move each note diatonically to the given scale or mode to reach the destination voicing:

EXAMPLE 5

Shifting is another common non-harmonic solution. As with the preceding example, visualize an arrival chord, but instead of planing through the mode, consider shifting the same chord quality one half step above or below the destination chord.

EXAMPLE 6

Left Hand

There is not much to say about the left hand, except that it doubles the top-note melody in traditional locked hands. However, some players add an occasional grace note in the left hand. It is also interesting to note that Oscar Peterson sometimes placed more weight on the left hand when playing locked-hands voicings.

Practical Example

The following excerpt from an Oscar Peterson transcription illustrates an effective use of locked-hands technique.

EXAMPLE 7

LESSON #67: POWER VOICINGS

I like to use the term **power voicing** to describe an effective jazz piano voicing technique that is used by many jazz pianists, including Red Garland, Gene Harris, Oscar Peterson, and others. The technique can be particularly effective at the climax of a solo, as a send-off to a drum solo, or any time you want a big sound to mimic the effect of a big-band shout chorus.

Left Hand

Where locked-hands voicings utilize four-note rootless voicings in the right hand, the power voicing technique utilizes four-note rootless voicings in the left hand. The most common chord factors are the 3rd, 5th, 7th, and 9th, although the 13th is sometimes used in lieu of the 5th.

EXAMPLE 1

Right Hand

Play an octave in the right hand and include a chord tone between the octave, about a 4th or 5th from the bottom note. As is evident in the next example, there may be more than one suitable chord tone to play between a given octave. Several power voicings are shown for a G13 chord in Example 2.

EXAMPLE 2

Rhythm

In most cases, both hands play the same rhythm. Depending on dynamic level and register, the effect can be subtle or very exciting. Red Garland often used the technique when playing the melody of a tune, and the technique also works great in the context of melodic riffs or repeating patterns:

EXAMPLE 3

Shifting and Tonicization

Half-step shifting or tonicization can be applied to power voicings. Play through Example 4 and note how effectively the chromatic harmonies embellish the underlying chords, G13 and C13.

EXAMPLE 4

LESSON #68: EXTENDED ALBERTI

The **Alberti bass** is an accompanimental technique associated with Domenico Alberti (c. 1710–1740), the first composer to use it widely. Played in the left hand, the accompaniment figure consists of broken triads, usually with the notes played in this order: lowest, highest, middle, highest. Although the Alberti technique is rarely (if ever) used in jazz, a similar technique I like to call **extended Alberti** can be effective in solo ballads.

Basics

Instead of using the root, 3rd, and 5th in a single octave as in traditional Alberti bass, open the hand and play the 3rd an octave higher. The resulting accompaniment might be described as rich and warm:

EXAMPLE 1

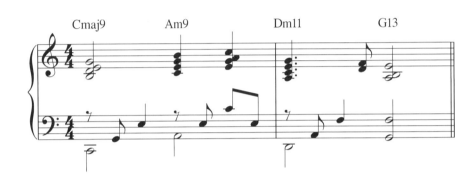

Using Non-harmonic Tones

Non-harmonic tones can be used to vary the pattern. I find it helpful to visualize such variations in a linear fashion. For example, notice how Example 2 takes on a more lyrical quality.

EXAMPLE 2

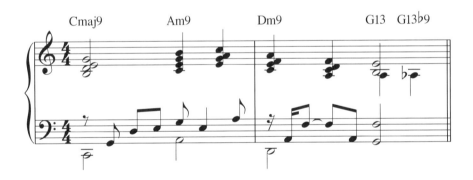

Rhythm

Jazz pianists often alter the rhythm of the left hand, as in Example 3. It may be helpful to practice the left hand separately in order to develop rhythmic and melodic fluency.

EXAMPLE 3

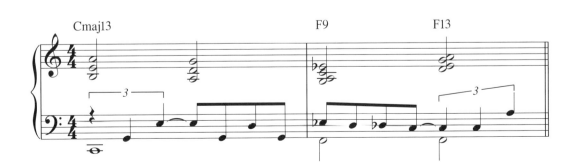

Practical Application

A beautiful example of extended Alberti can be heard on Bill Evans's recording of "Turn Out the Stars" from the *Bill Evans at Town Hall* album. You can also hear examples in his *Alone* album, as well as numerous other cuts.

EXAMPLE 1

A **pedal point** can be described as a sustained or repeating note that is played against changing harmonies. In jazz, pedal points are frequently heard in the bass register on the dominant. In this lesson we will explore several common applications of pedal points in jazz.

Percussive Pedal

Although many jazz pianists use pedal points, Nat Cole was one of the first jazz pianists to use them extensively in his solos. This approach, which might be described as a **percussive pedal**, is characterized by a low-register dominant pedal. Nat Cole often used an alternating octave with a grace note to embellish the top note of the octave. Example 1 is characteristic of his approach:

EXAMPLE 1

Harmonic Pedal

Pedal points are frequently used under ii-V or turnaround progressions, such as this:

EXAMPLE 2

Modal Pedal

Pedal points can also be effective in modal jazz. Pianists such as McCoy Tyner frequently employ them on the tonic under planing chords, as in Example 3:

EXAMPLE 3

Pedal Introductions and Endings

Pedal points can also be effective as an introduction or ending to a tune. Example 4, which is characteristic of a Basie introduction, demonstrates the approach:

EXAMPLE 4

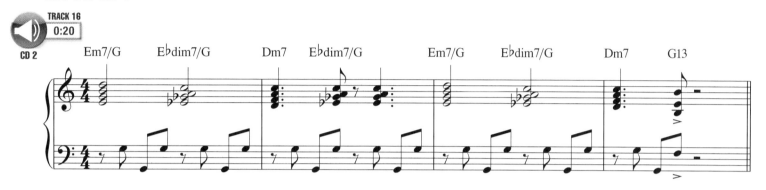

LESSON #70: TONICIZATION

Tonicization is a concept that I refer to in several lessons in this book. The concept is simple to describe, but can have profound implications in the realm of harmony. In this lesson, you will learn what tonicization is and how to incorporate the concept into your playing.

The descending Circle of 5ths progression is very strong in the Western European tradition. The strength of this harmonic motion is self-evident:

EXAMPLE 1

The effect is even more pronounced when major-minor 7th chords are used:

EXAMPLE 2

Tonicizing an Arrival Chord

Because the descending motion of a major-minor 7th chord is so strong, a major-minor 7th chord can be used to temporarily tonicize an arrival chord. For example, a G7 tends to want to move to a C chord, regardless of the key in which the G7 is heard. Classical theorists call such chords **secondary dominants** or **applied dominants**.

EXAMPLE 3

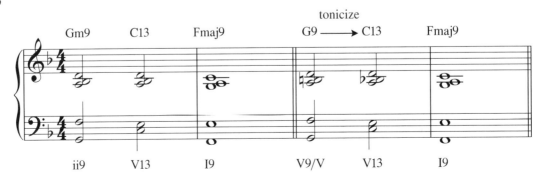

A tune such as "Isn't It Romantic" provides many opportunities for exploring tonicization. Play through Example 4 and consider the primary arrival chords. In general, an arrival chord can be thought of as the expected chord change at a given point in the tune. Next, consider how major-minor 7th chords could be inserted to tonicize the arrival chords. Example 5 demonstrates one possible approach.

EXAMPLE 4

EXAMPLE 5

Of course, the previous example might be considered somewhat over the top. A more traditional treatment might be in order. However, in order to thoroughly internalize a concept, it is often advisable to overdo the concept until it is second nature.

Other Enhancements

In many cases, an altered dominant or tritone substitute can be inserted in places where an applied dominant is effective. Similarly, tonicizing chord groups can be effective. For example, if V7 of a given chord can be inserted, it often works well to insert ii and V of the given arrival chord. Again, types of alterations should always be guided by tasteful treatment of the underlying song. The final except shows how the concept of tonicization, as well as applied altered chords and tritone substitutions, could be applied to "Isn't It Romantic."

EXAMPLE 6

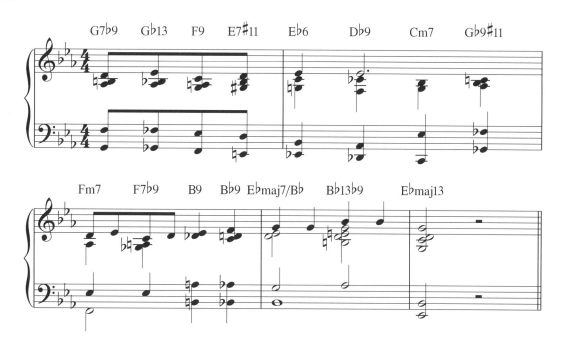

LESSON #71: TURNAROUND PROGRESSIONS

Turnaround progressions are a mainstay of most standard tunes and are typically heard in the last two bars of a tune. In this lesson, you will learn a number of harmonic techniques that can be utilized to make your turnarounds, and other progressions, more interesting.

Diatonic Turnaround

The most basic turnaround consists of diatonic chords that form a circle progression, either I-vi-ii-V or iii-vi-ii-V in a major key:

EXAMPLE 1

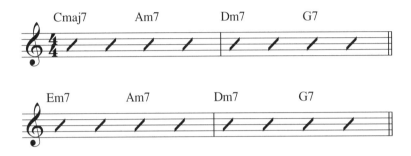

Tonicization

Applied or secondary dominants can enhance the sense of movement in the circle progression. Example 2 illustrates the theory behind this concept. Note that you might elect to change one or all of the chords, but the technique is effective only if the chords fit the given melody:

EXAMPLE 2

Altered Chords

If applied or secondary dominants fit with the existing melody, it may be possible to further enhance the progression by utilizing altered dominant chords, dominant chords with an altered 5th and/or altered 9th. As with the preceding example, it is not necessary to apply the concept to the entire progression.

EXAMPLE 3

Tritone Substitution

Instead of using applied or altered dominants, experiment with tritone substitution. Simply replace a given major-minor 7th chord with a major-minor 7th chord a tritone above or below the chord. It is helpful to note that the so-called Lydian dominant is the most common chord quality for a tritone substitute.

EXAMPLE 4

Turnaround Matrix

The concepts of diatonic circle progression, applied dominants, altered dominants, and tritone substitution can be combined to form what I like to call the **turnaround matrix**, a 4 x 4 matrix of options.

Em7	Am7	Dm7	G7
E7	A7	D7	G7
E7alt.	A7alt.	D7alt.	G7alt.
B♭7♯11	E♭7♯11	A♭7♯11	D♭7♯11

You might, for example, start with a diatonic selection, move to an applied dominant, incorporate a tritone substitute, and finish with another altered chord. According to my friend, mathematician Dr. Martha Gady, the potential variations can be described as 4 x 4 x 4 x 4 = 256 options. Clearly, there are many variations to explore! Example 5 illustrates just a few of the options.

EXAMPLE 5

LESSON #72: CHORD OF OMISSION

Classical theorists use the term **chord of omission** to describe chords in which one or more chord factors have been omitted. Chords of omission are useful to jazz pianists because they can be used to convey the color and function of a complex chord structure while maintaining a subtle and somewhat vague harmonic implication. In a word, it is up to the listener to fill in the missing notes. You can hear chords of omission in the music of Bill Evans, Keith Jarrett, Brad Mehldau, and others.

Common Chords of Omission

The trick to using chords of omission is to extract a two- or three-note structure from a complex voicing. For example, a common left-hand voicing for an A7#5(#9) voicing is shown below:

EXAMPLE 1

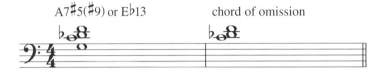

From this structure, a chord of omission consisting of the (enharmonic) notes C, Db, and F can be extracted. Not only can the grouping of notes be used to imply an A7 altered chord, the notes could be used to imply any number of other complex structures such as:

EXAMPLE 2

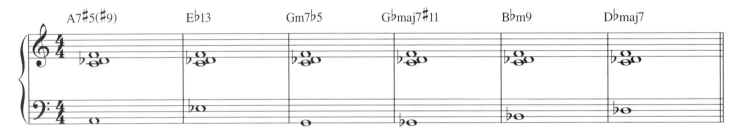

Another common chord of omission can be extracted from an Eb13 voicing:

EXAMPLE 3

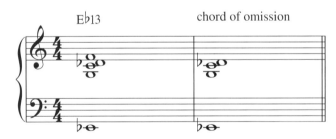

This voicing could be used to imply a number of chords, including those in Example 4.

EXAMPLE 4

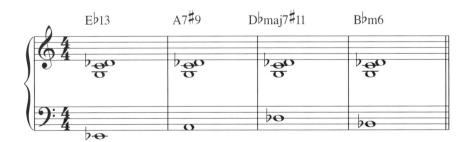

As you can see in the preceding examples, the most successful applications contain either the 3rd or 7th of the implied structure.

Practicing Chords of Omission

One way to practice chords of omission is to use the examples in this lesson as a theoretical key by which you can transpose the voicings to other keys. However, I have found that an intuitive approach can also be effective. With this approach, simply be open to the possibility of omitting a note from stock four-note left-hand voicings:

EXAMPLE 5

Practical Application

Example 6 illustrates one approach to utilizing chords of omission. Play through the example and listen to the subtle implication of harmony that is imparted by the voicings:

EXAMPLE 6

TRACK 18
0:00
CD 2

Three-note voicings are frequently used by jazz pianists. In this lesson you will learn some of the most common options as well as practice strategies that will enable you to play three-note voicings for a wide variety of tunes.

Why Three Notes?

I have noticed that some of the greatest jazz pianists use relatively simple three-note voicings on occasion. This begs the question "why?" In my estimation, three-note voicings are particularly useful in the left hand because three notes are just enough to imply almost any complex chord, but the simplicity of the voicings helps to keep them in the background. Not only are the voicings useful in jazz piano, the concepts in this lesson are readily applicable to writing arrangements for three horns.

Common Three-Note Voicings

The most common three-note voicings utilize the 3rd, 7th, and a color tone. Play through the following examples to get a feel for the voicings:

EXAMPLE 1

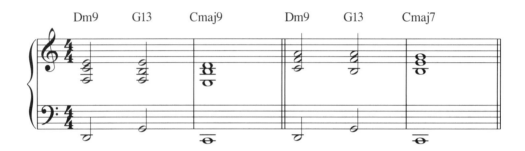

For major and minor 6/9 chords, the 6th can be used in place of the 7th:

EXAMPLE 2

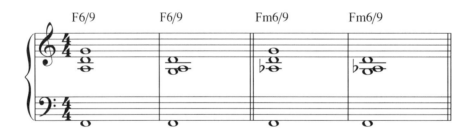

Leveraging Three-Note Voicings

It is worth pointing out that these voicings can often serve a dual purpose. For example, the G13 voicing shown in the first example also works as a three-note voicing for Dm6/9.

EXAMPLE 3

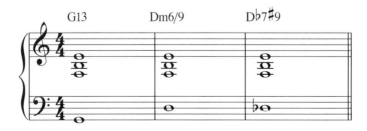

Altered Voicings

Three-note voicings can also be effective when voicing altered dominant chords. Simply play the 3rd and 7th and add an altered 5th or 9th, as in the next example:

EXAMPLE 4

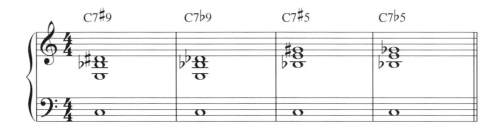

Voice Leading

The 3rd and 7th provide the key to smooth voice leading when playing three-note voicings. For this reason, it is helpful to practice playing just 3rds and 7ths for a given progression in order to familiarize your hands with the smoothest possible voice leading. Once you are comfortable playing 3rds and 7ths, it will be easy to add an additional color tone or altered tone as in Example 5:

EXAMPLE 5

LESSON #74: EXTENDED HARMONY

Jazz musicians tend to relish colorful harmony. Advanced harmony is such an important element that it could even be said that it is a distinguishing feature of the art form. In this lesson, you will learn about **extended harmony**, the harmonies that provide such a distinctive sound in jazz.

Extensions

The word tertian is used to describe harmony that is built in thirds. Tertian chords such as triads and 7th chords form the basis for most music in the Western European tradition. If you construct a chord in 3rds and continue past the 7th of the chord, you will find the chord extensions consisting of the 9th, 11th, and 13th:

EXAMPLE 1

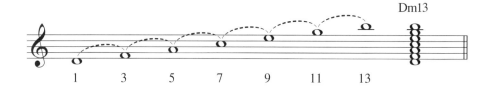

Chord Symbols

At first glance, chords like G♭13♯11 or Bm(maj9) might seem confusing, but the symbols that are used to describe extended harmonies follow a very simple system: The 9th and 13th are always major unless an alteration (+/- or ♯/♭) is specified. Similarly, the 11th is always perfect unless an alteration is specified. Let's look at the four common 7th chords to see how this works:

EXAMPLE 2

In the next illustration, a 9th has been added to each of the common 7th chords. Note how the underlying symbol does not change. For example, a Cm9 chord is a Cm7 with a major 9th added, and a C9 chord is a C7 with a major 9th added:

EXAMPLE 3

In Example 4, a 13th has been added to each chord. Again, notice how the underlying chord symbol remains unchanged: C13 is a C7 with a 9th and 13th added, and a Cmaj13 is a Cmaj7 with a major 9th and 13th added. Students sometimes ask why a 6th is listed with some chords and a 13th, the same note, with others. Example 4 provides a perfect illustration: The 13th indicates that the 7th (and optionally the 9th) are included, while a chord containing a 6th would not be extended and would consist of the root, 3rd, 5th, and an added 6th:

EXAMPLE 4

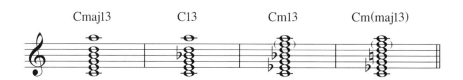

Chord Groups

I find it helpful to visualize extended harmonies in groups or palettes of related chords. This makes it convenient to visualize the types of spur-of-the-moment selections that jazz pianists make when harmonizing a tune. For example, a lead sheet for a tune like "Take the A Train" might list a C or C6 for the first chord change, but a mature jazz pianist might elect to use a C6/9, Cmaj9, or another option on any given chorus. Example 5 shows the most common extended harmonies in groups of related chords.

EXAMPLE 5

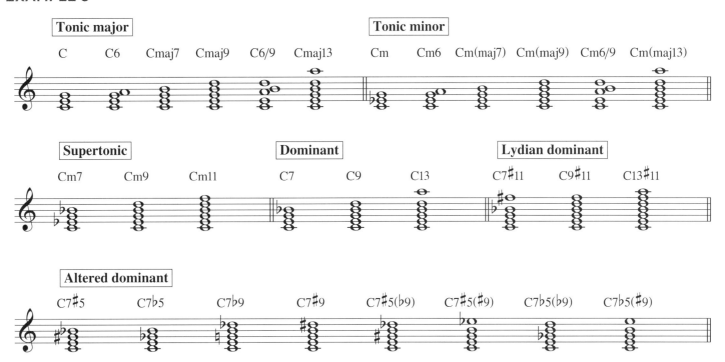

LESSON #75: LEFT-HAND COMPING

Since the advent of the modern era of jazz, most pianists utilize a left-hand accompaniment that is characterized by mid-register voicings and somewhat sparse rhythm. Developing an organic left hand can be particularly challenging for players that are new to jazz piano, so this lesson will focus on this important aspect of playing.

Conceptual Overview

It is often helpful to visualize the hands as representing two instruments. For example, the right-hand could be thought of as a saxophone solo, and the left-hand accompaniment might represent a guitar accompaniment. Just as two instrumentalists will try to complement each other when improvising, the left and right hands should have an independent yet complementary relationship.

Independence of Hands: Filling During Rests

For new jazz pianist, one of the challenges is often coordinating the left and right hands. One useful practice technique is to play the left hand only when the right hand is resting when playing a solo or the melody of a tune.

EXAMPLE 1

Independence of Hands: Repeating Pattern

Players such as Ahmad Jamal and Wynton Kelly sometimes use a repeating left-hand pattern or riff as in Example 2. Practicing similar patterns can help you to develop the necessary independence to effectively comp in your left hand underneath a right-hand solo.

EXAMPLE 2

Interdependence of Hands

Although the left hand sometimes functions in an independent fashion as in the last two examples, most left-hand comping relates in a more deliberate way to the right hand. Notice how Kenny Barron's left hand fits with the right hand in such a natural and complementary way:

EXAMPLE 3

Yet another approach is to use the same rhythm in both hands. This can be particularly effective during a climactic part of a solo such as the Bill Evans example below from "Waltz for Debby."

EXAMPLE 4

USING 3RDS AND 7THS IN THE LEFT HAND

Some pianists utilize sparse voicings consisting of **3rds and 7ths in the left hand** on occasion. Not only is the technique useful in providing contrast to more meaty voicings, 3rds and 7ths are building-block voicings that can contribute to better voice leading.

Implying Chords with 3 and 7

A voicing truism is that the 3rd and 7th of a chord provide the primary sound or identity of a chord. You can experiment with this idea by playing 3rds and 7ths over the root of a given chord. Although the voicings are simple, all the primary colors of the chords can be heard:

EXAMPLE 1

Voice Leading

When using 3rds and 7ths in either hand, be conscious of the proximity of the 3rd and 7th of adjacent chords. In many cases, minimal movement will be required to move from chord to chord. In this sense, 3rds and 7ths are a key to unlocking smooth voice leading. Example 2 illustrates how easy it is to play a typical progression of chords by being conscious of nearby chord tones.

EXAMPLE 2

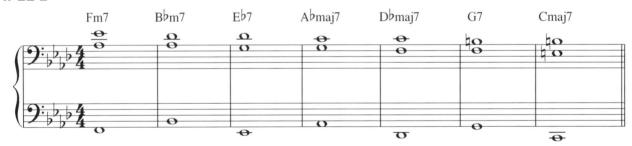

Practicing Turnaround Progressions

A turnaround progression provides a perfect vehicle for practicing smooth voice leading with 3rds and 7ths. Practice both versions of the following exercise in all keys:

EXAMPLE 3

Blues Inflection

Players such as Oscar Peterson frequently use 3rds and 7ths in the left hand when playing blues riffs or to provide a bluesy quality when tonicizing a turnaround progression. The following excerpt comes from "Falling in Love with Love."

EXAMPLE 4

LESSON #77: QUARTAL HARMONY

While most chords are built in 3rds (tertian harmony), it is also possible to construct chords from 2nds (secundal), 4ths (quartal), and 5ths (quintal). In this lesson, we will explore **quartal harmony**, an approach that is often associated with the music of McCoy Tyner.

Three-Note Quartal Voicing

Three-note quartal voicings are very common in the left hand behind a right-hand solo. One way to incorporate quartal voicings is to be conscious of chords that contain the notes of a given quartal structure. Such voicings tend to be particularly effective if one of the chord factors is the 3rd or 7th of the chord. Here are a few:

EXAMPLE 1

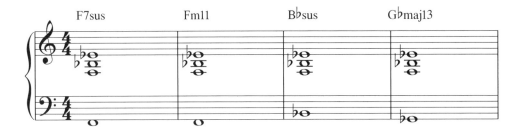

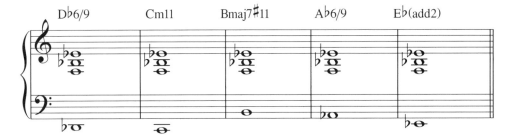

Inversions

It is also helpful to be aware that quartal inversions retain their modern quartal quality, even if the voicings don't look quartal:

EXAMPLE 2

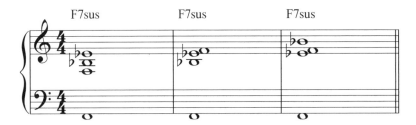

Four-Note Quartal Voicing

Four-note quartal voicings can be very effective when played behind a soloist. As with three-note voicings, experiment by applying quartal voicings to chords that contain the same chord factors:

EXAMPLE 3

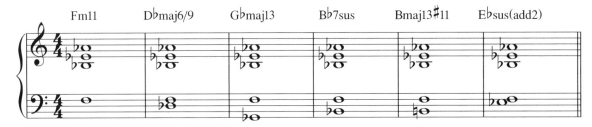

Hybrid Quartal/Tertian Voicing

The so-called "So What" voicing represents a category of voicing that might be described as a hybrid quartal/tertian voicing. Note how the chord consists primarily of the interval of a 4th with the interval of a 3rd between the top two voices. As with pure quartal voicings, many applications are possible:

EXAMPLE 4

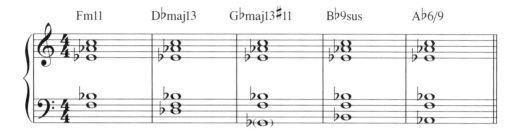

Modal Planing

Pianists such as McCoy Tyner frequently utilize diatonic planing in the context of playing quartal voicings. Example 5 demonstrates diatonic planing for an F minor (F Dorian) chord.

EXAMPLE 5

Playing Out

More than with tertian structures, quartal structures lend themselves to "playing out." In many cases, the "out" chord is a half step away from the current key or mode, and the tension of being close to (but out of) the key provides a wonderful sense of impetus to the destination key or mode.

EXAMPLE 6

One of my favorite musical activities is to play through J.S. Bach's four-part chorales. They are a marvel of impeccable voice leading and harmonic inventiveness. Today, jazz pianists and arrangers often use a similar process when harmonizing a ballad. In this lesson, we will look at a number of strategies that can help you to utilize good voice leading and to create effective voicings.

Why Five Notes?

Where three notes are just enough to imply a basic chord quality, five notes are often used to create harmonically rich structures that are associated with a typical jazz ballad. Although these tips are written in the context of book of jazz piano lessons, I would stress that the concepts are also applicable to orchestral and choral arranging and composition.

Voicing Tips

Although the voicing steps listed in this lesson might seem overly pedantic, the tips will generally produce voicings that are rich and satisfying. A first step is to select one of the following structures in the left hand.

1. Place the root as the lowest voice and add one of the following intervals above the root:
   - Root & 7th (Root-7th will sound muddy in low registers.)
   - Root & 10th
   - Root & 5th
   - Octave (Don't use octaves for extended chords; they tend to overpower.)
   - Root-6th (Use a 6th only for major 6th or minor 6th chords.)
   - Root & 3rd can work if the voicing is not too low.

2. Place the melody note as the highest sounding note.

3. Add the 3rd and/or 7th as needed.

4. Add color (e.g., 9th, 11th, 13th as appropriate). Don't place color tones in the bass register.

5. Avoid gaps >= 7th between voices. (Note that a large gap is desirable between the lowest two voices.)

6. Avoid a semitone between the top two notes. (Half-steps are fine between alto and tenor voices.)

7. Omit the 5th when necessary.

The following demonstrates how the preceding steps could be utilized to voice several chords.

EXAMPLE 1

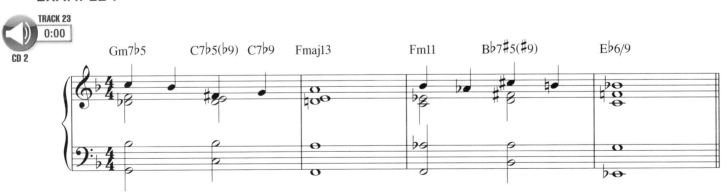

Voice-Leading Tips

Vertical voicing is only one part of the process of creating successful harmonizations. **Voice leading**, the smooth transition of one note to the next, is also important. The following tips are a useful starting point.

1. Use common tones when possible, except for the bass.

2. Consider voice-leading in tenor voice first (i.e., all chords should not be voiced over the same building block interval).

3. Use tendency tones (e.g., the lowered 9th of an altered dominant tends to resolve down and augmented 5ths tend to resolve up).

4. The 7th of a dominant tends to resolve down.

5. Parallel perfect consonances are fine in this genre.

6. Contrary motion is desirable when possible.

The following five-part harmonization of "I Can't Get Started" demonstrates how the tips in this lesson could be applied to a standard tune. Note the use of rich harmonies, smooth voice leading, a variety of left-hand structures, and the fact that the melody is always in the top voice.

EXAMPLE 2

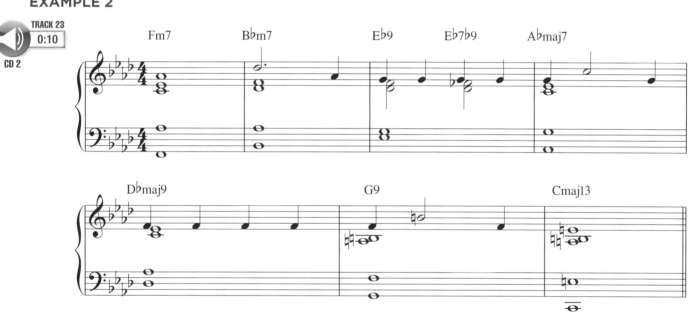

LESSON #79: BOOGIE-WOOGIE

Boogie-woogie represents an interesting offshoot of jazz that is purely pianistic. Although the relationship of boogie-woogie to jazz is somewhat akin to the relationship of disco to rock 'n' roll, boogie formed the basis for some later popular genres, including rockabilly. Boogie-woogie tracks such as those performed by Meade Lux Lewis, Albert Ammons, and others are characterized by a repeating left-hand pattern, blues form, and frequent blues licks and cross-rhythms in the right hand.

Left-Hand Patterns Utilizing the Root and 5th

A number of common left hand patterns utilize the root and 5th, as in the following examples.

EXAMPLE 1–3

Left-Hand Patterns Utilizing Outlines

Another common approach to the left hand is to outline chords with alternating octaves:

EXAMPLE 4–5

Adding the Right Hand

Part of the fun, and challenge, of playing boogie-woogie is adding an independent right hand. Such independence can be fostered by using a repeating riff based on the blues scale or chord tones. It will be possible to add cross rhythms and other blues elements as you get comfortable playing repeating patterns, as in the next example:

EXAMPLE 6

TRACK 24
0:00
CD 2

Practical Application

The final excerpt demonstrates how blues concepts such as a repeating left hand, blues scales, and riffs could be applied to a 12-bar boogie-woogie blues.

EXAMPLE 7

ROOTLESS VOICINGS

Rootless voicings are some of the most-used voicings in jazz. Jazz pianists often use them in the left hand to accompany a right-hand solo, and they provide a foundation for a number of other voicing techniques, including locked-hands voicings, power voicings, and drop-2 voicings. In this lesson, we will explore a number of concepts that will enable you to utilize this important category of harmony.

What Are Rootless Voicings?

As the name implies, rootless voicings are those in which the root has been omitted. Although rootless voicings might seem counterintuitive at first glance, the root is not always necessary because complex chords are often implied in context with other chords. In Example 1, for instance, the key and harmonic progression are implied even though roots are not used in the bass register. This is akin to deciphering the meaning of an unfamiliar word because of its context in a sentence.

EXAMPLE 1

TRACK 25
0:00
CD 2

Adding the 9th and 13th

The 9th and 13th are two tones that are frequently added to chords to provide color. A common rule of thumb in rootless voicing is that the 9th can be added in lieu of the root, and the 13th can be used in place of the 5th. Since the 9th and 13th are adjacent to the root and 5th respectively, it is easy to add these color tones to any voicing (e.g., simply move the root up a whole step to add the 9th to a chord).

EXAMPLE 2

It is important to note that this process works for any inversion:

EXAMPLE 3

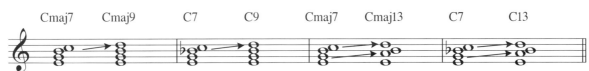

Altered Tones

As with color tones, altered tones can be utilized in the context of rootless voicing. In Example 4, altered 5ths and 9ths are added to major-minor 7th chords to create a stronger sense of movement to an arrival chord:

EXAMPLE 4

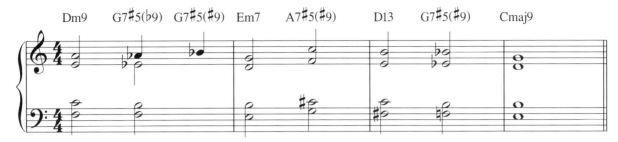

Adding the 11th

When voicing rootless chords, the 11th is often added in lieu of the 5th. Note that the perfect 11th sounds good only as a color tone on minor chords, but the raised 11th is sometimes used with major 7th and major-minor 7th chords.

EXAMPLE 5

Voicing Concepts

Four-note rootless voicings can form the foundation for a number of other voicing concepts that are discussed in other lessons in this book. Here are a few of the most common applications:

EXAMPLE 6

LESSON #81: USING DIMINISHED SCALES

The **diminished scale**, also called an **octatonic scale**, is frequently heard in jazz and contemporary classical music. The scale is interesting because it consists solely of whole and half steps. It is also interesting to note that the scale contains two diminished 7th chords:

EXAMPLE 1

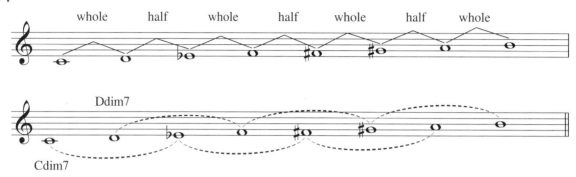

Diminished Chords

As you might expect from the name of the scale, the diminished scale is a good choice as a scale resource for a diminished 7th chord. The whole-step/half-step form of the scale is typically used:

EXAMPLE 2

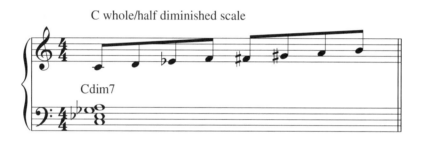

Altered Chords

Diminished scales are also used for a specific type of altered dominant that is characterized by a major 13th and a lowered 9th. It is important to stress that the half-step/whole-step form of the scale is used. In fact, the diminished scale contains the root, altered 9ths, 3rd, 5th, raised 11th, 13th, and 7th of the chord:

EXAMPLE 3

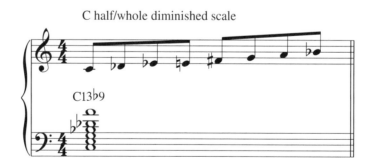

Practicing Diminished Scales

The good news about diminished scales is that there are only three scales to learn. Due to the symmetrical nature of the scale, a C diminished scale contains the same notes as the E♭, G♭, and A diminished scale:

EXAMPLE 4

Players often utilize symmetrical patterns when improvising with a diminished scale. Practice the following etudes in each of the three possible diminished scale transpositions to familiarize yourself with the melodic potential of the scale.

EXAMPLE 5

Practical Application

It is always useful to see how a scale like the diminished scale might be used "in the wild." The following transcription is from a Kenny Barron recording.

EXAMPLE 6

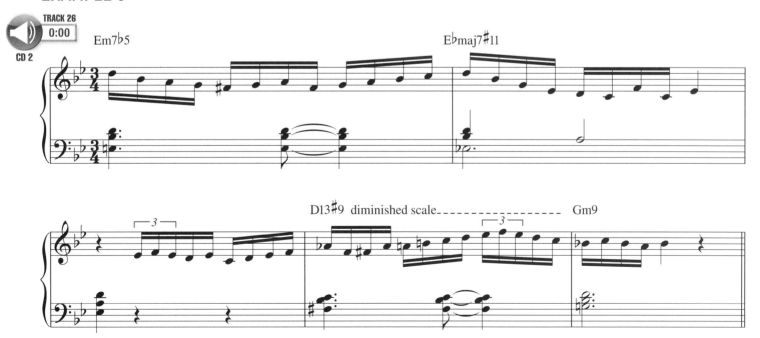

The concept of **swing** is a tricky thing to describe with prose. Unlike classical music, where there tends to be at least a general agreement with the primary parameters of style and articulation, the parameters of jazz style are not as well defined. Part of reason for this lack of clarity has to do with the fact that individual style has always been an important characteristic of this truly American art form: Independence and individuality are two of the characteristics that differentiate jazz from classical music.

Eighth Notes

When jazz musicians talk about swing rhythms, they are generally referring to the practice of "swinging" the eighth notes. In most cases, the following notation is close to an ideal interpretation of swinging eighth notes:

EXAMPLE 1

Why Aren't Jazz Rhythms Notated as Played?

Students sometimes ask why jazz rhythms are not notated correctly, as in the previous example. My response is usually that such notation would be needlessly complex. It is also helpful to recognize that rhythmic shorthand is used in many other styles of music. For example, the dotted rhythms associated with French overture are sometimes modified in performance, and string players are accustomed to interpreting "slash" notation that is used to indicate various divisions and subdivisions of the beat.

Eighth Notes and Tempo

Although the preceding triplet notation is generally correct, it is important to note that the space between eighth notes usually varies depending on tempo. A general rule of thumb is that swing eighths are "wider" a slower tempos. One way to visualize this relationship is to consider the space between swing eighths on a sliding scale with dotted-eighth and 16th representing slow tempos and even or straight-eighth notes representing fast tempos. Although other factors come into play (swing-eighth notes tend to be wider in the swing era, for example), a sliding scale of eighth-note widths is a useful way to visualize swing rhythms.

EXAMPLE 2

Rhythmic Signature

It is not always necessary for all players in a combo to agree on the same approach to swing rhythms. Although extreme variance would probably detract from an underlying groove, the music can still swing if players bring different interpretations to the table. I have heard this variance described as a rhythmic signature, and it is interesting to pay attention to subtle differences in swing conception when listening to recordings. Of course, this concept is moot if players are playing a unison line; it would be important for players to play such a line with the same rhythmic interpretation.

Slurs and Articulation

Rhythm isn't the only musical element that contributes to swing. Slurs and articulation are also important. To see how this works, play the following passage at a fast tempo slurring all the notes:

EXAMPLE 3

Play the passage again at a fast tempo and add the following accents:

EXAMPLE 4

Play the excerpt once more and add the following slurs and articulations. You will likely hear that, even though the rhythms are performed using straight eighths, the slurs and articulations contribute to a sense of swing.

EXAMPLE 5

Learning How to Swing

Although we have considered several important aspects of swing style, the only way to learn to swing, and utilize appropriate slurs and articulation, is to listen to lots of jazz. Although there are many jazz pianists that are known for their ability to swing, I always encourage students to absorb the swing conception of the Count Basie Orchestra. The ensemble is widely admired for its ability to swing, and you will be able to swing with the best if you absorb some of Basie's recordings.

INTRODUCTION TO RHYTHM CHANGES

The term **rhythm changes** refers to the progression of chords for George Gershwin's "I Got Rhythm." A number of well-known bebop melodies including "Moose the Mooche" and "Thriving from a Riff" were written to be played over the same set of changes as the original tune.

Chord Progression

Rhythm changes follows an AABA form with the A sections being largely comprised of a turnaround progression. However, the movement to the IV chord in bar 6 is an important arrival point. The first two A sections are shown below.

EXAMPLE 1

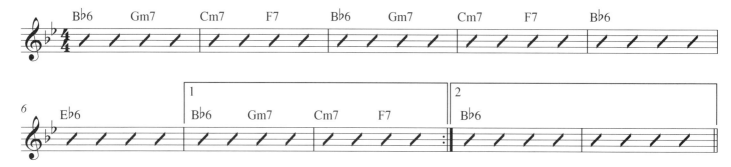

The bridge follows a descending circle progression (each chord is a perfect 5th lower than the preceding chord). The progression starts on III in the key and continues around the Circle of 5ths:

EXAMPLE 2

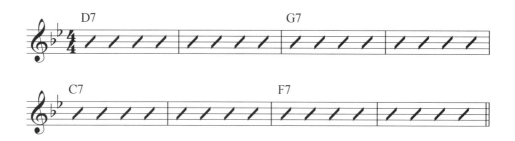

The entire progression is shown in Example 3. As with blues progressions, there are many variations, such as using temporary ii-Vs on the bridge (e.g., Am7-D7, Dm7-G7, etc.) or using secondary dominants on the A sections (e.g. Bb-G7-Cm7-F7).

EXAMPLE 3

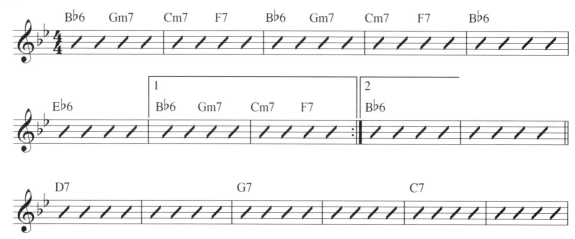

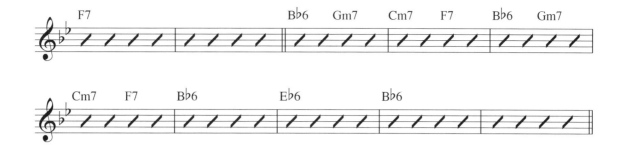

Chord and Scale Relationships

Although most players utilize a preponderance of chord tones when improvising on rhythm changes, it is helpful to understand the underlying chord and scale relationships. The tonic major scale is usually the best, and most obvious choice, over the A section for riffs or other melodic ideas that are superimposed over the progression of chords. In contrast, Mixolydian or bebop scales are a good choice for the bridge. The ♯11 is also an interesting note choice that can be heard on many recordings.

EXAMPLE 4

Improvising on Rhythm Changes

Rhythm changes are primarily associated with bebop, so one of the most effective techniques is to utilize chord tones and embellishments such as neighbor tones, changing tones, and passing tones. The following excerpt from a Charlie Parker solo on "Moose the Mooche" illustrates a number of these concepts.

EXAMPLE 5

Transcription from *Charlie Parker Omnibook*

Another helpful technique is to utilize the 3rd, 5th, 7th, and lowered 9th of the dominant and secondary dominants as a melodic unit. Notice how these tones effectively convey the chord progression:

EXAMPLE 6

Jazz pianists are frequently called upon to create an on-the-spot **introduction** to a tune, so it is an important skill to develop in order to be ready for gigging opportunities. In this lesson we will look at several tips that will provide a useful starting point in creating effective introductions.

Establish the Key

When in doubt, one of the most effective introduction strategies is simply to establish the key. A ii-V or I-vi-ii-V progression can be effective:

EXAMPLE 1

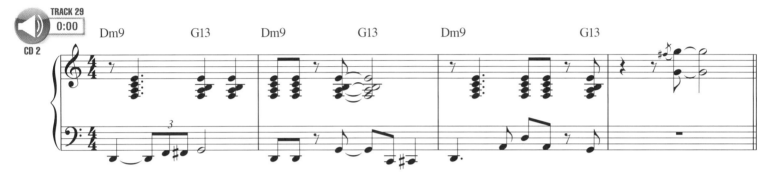

Pedal Point

Pedal points can be used to provide a slightly different effect. A pedal point on the dominant works well under a ii-V or I-vi-ii-V progression:

EXAMPLE 2

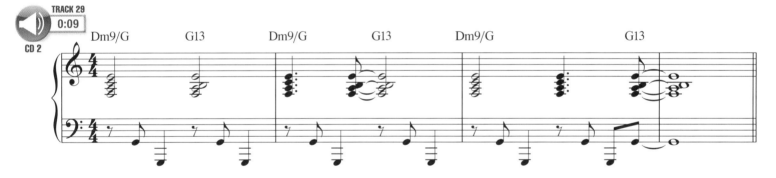

Third Relation

A nice variation on the dominant pedal is to use establish the key, move a minor 3rd higher, and then return to the original key:

EXAMPLE 3

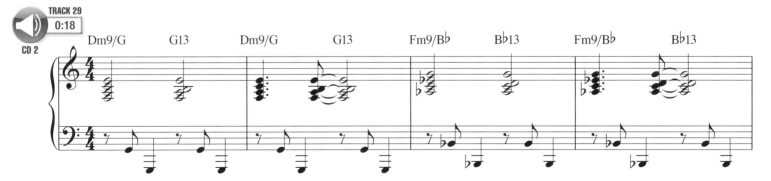

Paraphrase the Tune

Another common way to approach an introduction is to paraphrase the last four or eight bars of the tune, as in Example 4:

EXAMPLE 4

Vamp

A repeating vamp can be useful as an introduction. Of course, progressions like ii-V or a turnaround can work well, but a descending whole step vamp or other repeating pattern can also be effectual. For example, an ascending half-step vamp is very common on Latin tunes.

EXAMPLE 5

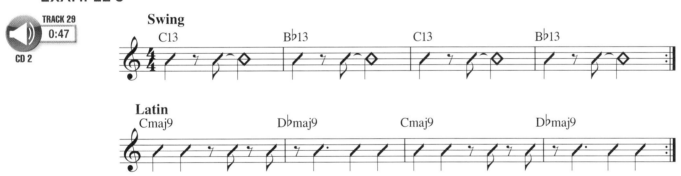

Establish the Wrong Key and Modulate

One of my favorite introduction techniques for a ballad is to establish a distant key (one that is several sharps or flats away from the original key) and modulate to the correct key at the end of the introduction. The unexpected use of a modulation can help the tune to sound very fresh:

EXAMPLE 6

LESSON #85: ENDINGS

Jazz pianists are often called upon to set up an on-the-fly **ending** to a tune in the context of a jam session of or jazz "casual." In this lesson, we will explore a number of techniques that can help you to steer a combo to a successful, if unrehearsed, conclusion to a tune.

Basie Endings

Although it is now considered a cliché, a jazz pianist should be able to play the following Basie endings in any key should the need arise. These endings are the musical equivalent of shouting, "We are ending the tune now!"

EXAMPLE 1

Vamp and Ritard

A vamp such as the following can provide an effective ending to a tune. An ascending half step or descending whole step almost always works well as a vamp, but other options such as I-IV are also effective.

EXAMPLE 2

Getting Out of a Vamp

The only problem with an on-the-fly vamp ending is that it can be difficult to get out of the vamp. I have noticed that an ascending quarter note line can provide an effective signal to the other members of a combo that the vamp will slow into a fermata:

EXAMPLE 3

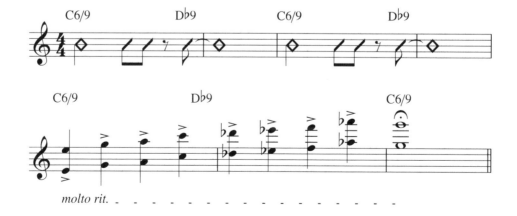

Extended Turnaround

Many jazz musicians utilize turnaround vamps at the conclusion of a tune. From a pianist's perspective, the primary consideration is to utilize a chord to signal the turnaround. In most cases, this involves inserting V7/ii or using a descending half-step progression in place of the expected tonic chord, as in the following:

EXAMPLE 4

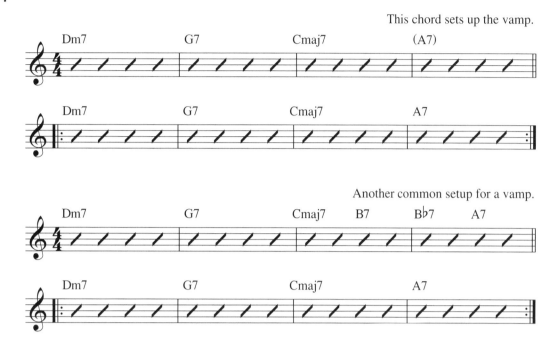

Raised IV Diminished

One of my favorite endings is to move to the raised IV diminished and utilize the following progression of chords. This is one of my go-to progressions when I want a slightly out-of-the-ordinary ending in the context of a jam session or casual:

EXAMPLE 5

IV Chord and Out

Another nice ending is to use V7/IV at the end of a tune to set up the following ending:

EXAMPLE 6

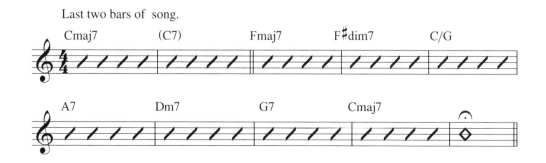

CREATING AN ARRANGEMENT

Functioning as an effective jazz pianist involves more than playing effective chords, rhythms, and solos. Most well-known jazz pianists also develop trademark **arrangements** of standard tunes. In fact, it could be said that developing unique and interesting arrangements is one of the most important aspects of playing in a jazz piano trio.

Establishing a Vibe

I find it helpful to think in terms of establishing a **vibe**. For example, an interesting re-harmonization or vamp might set the tone for the arrangement or the arrangement might evolve out of a unique rhythmic twist or interplay between the piano, bass, and drums. There is no "correct" way to approach a tune, so be open to possibilities and allow yourself the time to explore a standard tune from a number of angles.

Cohesion

Once you establish a unique vibe or "hook," consider how the element can be used to provide **cohesion** throughout the arrangement. For example, a unique pedal point might be inserted at the end of each iteration of the tune or a recurring rhythmic element could be used to unify the arrangement.

Form

Although it is usually best to honor the underlying tune by utilizing key elements of the melody and harmony, it is sometimes effective to alter the **form**. Common variations might include a vamp interlude between choruses, a shout-chorus send off to a drum solo, modulation of a part of the tune, extended ending, or other variation.

Example

The following outline of "Over the Rainbow" shows one way of adding a distinctive element to a well-known tune. In this example, a hook consisting of an ascending progression – shown on page 175 – provides a unique and unifying element to the arrangement.

Hook	A1	Short hook	A2	Bridge	A3	Hook 3x	Solos & out

It is important to **memorize** songs if you intend to do gigs and jam sessions as a jazz musician. It is impossible to know *every* tune, but it is important to know *some* tunes. In this lesson we will explore a number of concepts that will enable you to memorize songs more easily and to play them in a variety of keys.

Melody

When it comes to memorizing songs, the **melody** is your biggest ally. The melody provides many clues to the chord progression and provides the roadmap of the form. For this reason, I always focus on internalizing the melody when learning a new song. A good first step is to vocalize the melody until you can sing it from memory. Not only will singing help you to remember the melody, vocalization will allow you to play the song in other keys. Once you can sing the melody, use some theory to simplify the process of playing the melody on the piano. The standard tune "Autumn Leaves" provides a good example. Notice how the melody starts on "la" (6 in B♭ major, 1 in G minor) and ascends up the scale with a jump to "fa" (4 in B♭ major, 6 in G minor).

EXAMPLE 1

The remainder of the A section consists of a sequence: The initial idea is played again on the next note in the scale. These three bits of information (play a scale starting on la, jump to fa, and sequence on the next note in the key) will allow you to play the tune in any key.

EXAMPLE 2

Similarly, it is very easy to play a song like "Night and Day" if you remember that the melody starts on sol (5 in the key) and consists of a descending scale with a chromatic lower neighbor tone below the 3rd of the chord. The second phrase primarily consists of a descending chromatic line starting from mi (3 in the key). Play (and sing) the following excerpt and see if you can transpose it to other keys.

EXAMPLE 3

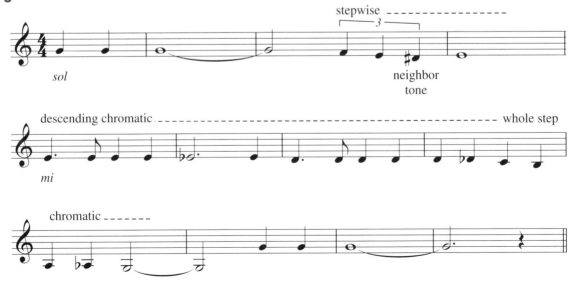

Chord Progressions

Most **chord progressions** for standard tunes are easy to memorize if you know what is, and isn't, important. Essential elements consist of primary arrival points, temporary key centers, and other distinctive harmonic principles. In general, turnaround progressions and "filler" chords – the chords that connect primary arrival points – are not as essential and can often be intuited by knowing the primary arrival points. For example, the first section of "Autumn Leaves" can be summarized this way: ii-V-I in a major key, ii-V-i in the relative minor. There is a pivot chord, E♭ in Example 4, to connect the major and relative minor, but it is less important.

EXAMPLE 4

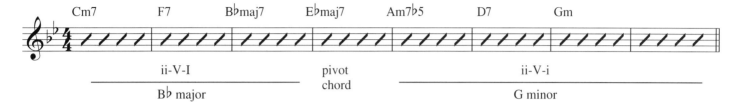

Similarly, the A section of "Honeysuckle Rose" can be visualized as a series of ii-V progressions in the major key, followed by a turnaround.

EXAMPLE 5

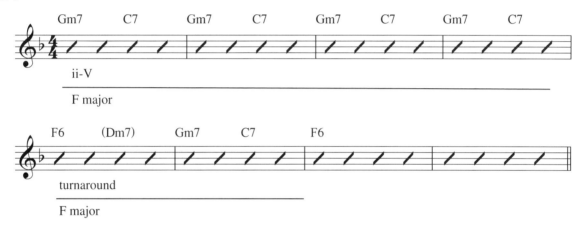

The bridge is also easy to visualize with this type of *CliffsNotes* approach: The tonic chord turns into V7/IV and is followed by V7/V.

EXAMPLE 6

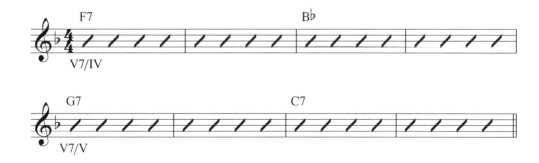

The good news is that, once you start memorizing songs in this way, it will be easy to learn and memorize new tunes. You will likely notice a snowball effect that will enable you to expand your repertoire of songs and to be able to play many of the songs in a variety of keys.

LESSON #88: UTILIZING UPPER STRUCTURES IN A SOLO

Although the concept of upper structures is typically associated with advanced playing techniques, utilization of upper structures can often simplify the process of improvising over a set of chord changes. In this lesson, we will look at several strategies that will help you incorporate upper structures in your playing. The concepts can help your playing sound more organic and melodic, and the approach will help foster the type of melodic vocabulary associated with a modern playing style.

What Are Upper Structures?

With regard to extended harmony, the term **upper structure** refers to triads and 7th chords that are superimposed over another triad or 7th chord. A fairly obvious example is the fact that the 9th, raised 11th, and 13th of a Cmaj13#11 or C13#11 form a D-major triad. Less obvious is the fact that the raised 5th, root, and raised 9th of a C7#5(#9) form an Ab-major triad. The following illustration lists a number of upper structures to help you start visualizing chords in this way.

EXAMPLE 1

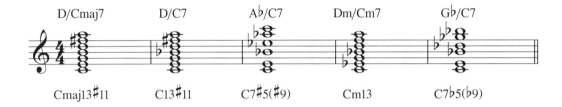

Relating Upper Structures to Chords and Scales

Upper structures can be intuited through experimentation, or you can use a more theoretical approach. One way to utilize theory is to recognize that triads and 7th chords can be constructed from a given chord/scale relationship, and the triads and 7ths can be used as upper structures, as in Example 2:

EXAMPLE 2

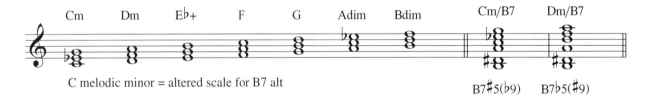

Guide Tones Expanded: Connection Chords

The concept of a guide tone line was presented in the lesson on utilizing chord tones in an improvisation, and a similar process can be applied to the concept of upper structures. Notice how the triads can be used to connect, and simplify, the following progression of chords. The triads can provide a simple, yet harmonically advanced, foundation for improvisation.

EXAMPLE 3

Here is another series of connecting chords for the same progression:

EXAMPLE 4

TRACK 32
0:00
CD 2

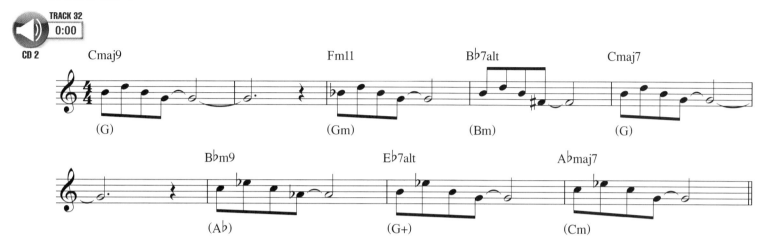

Practical Application

Example 5 comes from a Kenny Barron performance on "Delores Street, S.F." It is hard to know if the concept of upper structures informed the improvisation, but it is clear that the sound of upper structure triads was in Mr. Barron's ear.

EXAMPLE 5

TRACK 32
0:13
CD 2

Most jazz pianists use inner-voice movement when playing ballads (and other tunes), and it could be said that this type of linear motion is a characteristic of a mature jazz pianist. In this lesson we will explore a concept I like to call **inner-outer** that can help you to develop this important aspect of playing.

A Third Dimension

In the context of a jazz trio, a typical jazz piano solo often consists of an improvised line in the right hand over comping chords in the left hand. This type of two-dimensional approach can be heard on thousands of recordings and is certainly a mainstay of modern jazz piano technique. However, most players occasionally utilize a more linear approach that might be described as three dimensional. This is particularly true on ballads. One way to visualize this approach is to think of the inner fingers of both hands as sharing the role of providing harmony and rhythm while the outer fingers of the right and left hands provide melody and bass function respectively. I have heard this approach described as having a third hand, and I think that is apt.

Inner-Outer Right Hand

One way to practice the inner-outer concept is to play a melody with the outer fingers of the right hand while playing an accompaniment with the inner fingers. As with playing a Brahms intermezzo or Chopin prelude, focus on bringing the melody to the foreground while keeping the accompaniment in the background.

EXAMPLE 1

Inner-Outer Left Hand

A similar approach can be used in the left hand. In Example 2, note how the outer fingers of the left hand provide the bass function while the inner fingers provide an accompaniment. This type of linear approach is used by many jazz pianists.

EXAMPLE 2

Combining Hands

It will be possible to combine the hands in a linear approach once you are comfortable with the inner-outer concept in each hand separately. Play through the following excerpt and notice how the inner parts of the hand create a wonderful sense of depth to the passage by maintaining rhythmic and melodic independence from the melody and bass function.

EXAMPLE 3

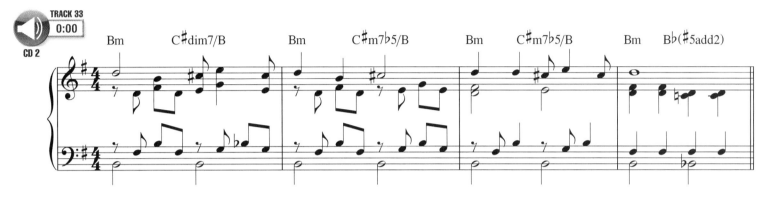

Practical Application

The following excerpt comes from a Bill Evans recording of "Turn Out the Stars." The recording features many examples of what might be described as a three-handed approach to playing.

EXAMPLE 4

LESSON #90: COMPING CONCEPTS

Although it is important to learn to be an effective soloist, my experience has been that jazz pianists are often hired for their ability to accompany. In fact, my working mantra is to try to *make other musicians sound great*. In this lesson, you will learn about a number of concepts that will help you develop this essential aspect of musicianship.

Function of a Jazz Pianist in an Ensemble

A jazz pianist has two primary functions in a jazz combo or jazz ensemble: to work with the bass player and drummer (and other rhythm-section musicians) to provide a harmonic and rhythmic underlayment. Although the pianist often takes a lead in harmonic function and the drummer often takes the lead in rhythm, it is important to note that the players share these functions and the relationship should be complementary. The bass player might take leading role in harmony or the pianist might provide the primary rhythmic direction at different points during a performance of a tune. It is also important for the pianist to listen to, and respond to, the soloist.

I once heard jazz pianist Hal Galper speak on the subject. He had a great way of describing the interconnected aspect of comping: The pianist should respond rhythmically to a soloist "through the ears of the drummer." In a similar way, the bass player might make a harmonic response to a solo "through the ears of the pianist."

Comping Resources

There are a number of primary comping resources available to a jazz pianist. Although these elements are obvious, it can be easy to forget how a simple element like dynamics or rhythm can contribute to, or detract from, a performance.

DYNAMICS

Dynamics are one of the easiest and most effective musical elements to incorporate in your accompaniments. (And dynamics are also one of the elements that are easy to forget about in a performance.) In many cases, a jazz pianist will follow the dynamic contour of a soloist, but it is sometimes appropriate for the pianist to lead. For example, the pianist might affect a diminuendo in the last four bars of a solo to signal the start of a new solo or new section of a tune. Similarly, a jazz pianist might dig in during a riff to encourage the rhythm section to lock in a groove.

RHYTHM

Be aware that a wide spectrum of rhythms is available to an accompanist. For example, long-note values or hemiolas can contribute to the floaty feeling of an introspective melodic solo, while more active rhythms and riffs might be effective behind a bluesy solo on a shuffle. Always be sure to work with the other members of the rhythm section when experimenting in the rhythmic domain. The best grooves and accompaniments are usually those in which the rhythm section works together in a complementary way. For example, the best complement to an active drum groove might be a fairly sparse accompaniment, while a repeating riff is often fits in nicely with a grooving shuffle. Also be aware that space can be an important ally. One of the most effective texture changes is simply to lay out for 16 or 32 bars when moving from the end of one solo to the start of another.

VOICING

Effective jazz pianists will have many voicing techniques under their fingers. For example, drop-2 voicings provide a relatively open sound that might be described as modern and subtle. In contrast, locked-hands voicings can provide a raw or "dirty" vibe when voiced in the baritone register of the piano. Also be conscious of the fact that simple voicings consisting of a 3rd and 7th or root and 10th can provide a nice contrast to more complex structures.

REGISTER

It is easy to get in a habit of playing voicings in the mid-range of the piano. While it is true that the middle register of the piano is the most common, and often the most appropriate, register for voicing, be sure to explore other registers. The baritone register just below middle C can provide a meaty accompaniment to a blues solo and the upper register is frequently used to accompany a bass solo. Extreme registers can also be effective if used judiciously: Duke Ellington sometimes played unison figures on the outer octaves of the instrument when accompanying a melody or solo, for example.

Vocalization

I once had the opportunity to do a few gigs with Chuck Israels, and I recall that he talked about vocalizing accompaniments when comping on the piano. That concept really resonated with me and helped me to develop a more mature approach to accompanying. One way to approach this concept is to visualize your comping as a saxophone or trombone section in a jazz ensemble. In a jazz ensemble, background parts are typically organized into comfortable phrase lengths and feature a fair amount of repetition. I have noticed that vocalization can contribute to a better balance between predictability and inventive interaction when accompanying a soloist.

Big-Picture Concepts

It is sometimes helpful to visualize the process of playing jazz as "collective composition." Where a well-crafted composition will have points of tension and relaxation as well as a feeling of inevitability, a well-crafted accompaniment can contribute to these same ideals. For this reason, strive to be aware of the primary comping elements including dynamics, rhythm, voicing, and register, and incorporate these elements in a way that contributes to a cohesive whole as the piece unfolds. In a word, most successful performances have a textural and density contour that might be described as dynamic rather than static.

LESSON #91: CALL AND RESPONSE

A common pattern of musical phrasing, especially in the African-American tradition, is **call and response**. The term stems from the kind of situation in which one singer, or leader, routinely puts forth a short line of a song – perhaps a question – and is answered by a chorus or congregation. But the influence of this phenomenon can be felt in other formats. Many a blues tune is written such that the first two-thirds of the 12-bar form both contain the same phrase (or similar), and the melodic line of the last four-bar segment answers the first two, with words as well as tones.

This kind of pattern also takes place in instrumental and improvised music and can inspire a certain way of shaping things even in our individual jazz solos. In general, it's good that one phrase or idea seems to follow the previous one naturally, giving a sense of melodic development, but you can take this a step further and try for a conversation with yourself in your own improvisation.

Structurally, this could happen in different ways. It doesn't need to be in the context of a 12-bar blues, but some kind of symmetrical form is helpful, like so many tunes have – with four- or eight-bar sections that can easily be divided into one-, two-, or four-bar chunks for our call and response.

Here's an example of one way to do this on a blues form (in the key of B♭), where each third of it is treated as a miniature three-phrase unit. That is, a short, rhythmically similar phrase is played in each of the first two measures, while the next two measures contain a longer line that seems to answer the first two This whole plan repeats for both of the remaining four-bar sections.

EXAMPLE 1

Throughout most of this example, an effort is made to choose tones that fit the chord changes, though the very last phrase is an exception, with some earthier blues scale material that skates through the chords, in a stylistically fitting way. This last phrase also goes on a bit longer and gives a sense of conclusion by the end of the 12-bar form. Even if we've had the same essential four-bar call-and-response pattern three times in a row, the third of these seems to answer the first eight measures altogether, neatly wrapping up one chorus of the blues.

In fact, the whole thing comes across like a bit of jazz-blues melody, and a similar approach has often been used to improvise an actual "head" (melody) for a blues-form tune in the style. This is frequently done with a simpler riff that is played once each for the first two four-bar chunks and answered in the last four measures, giving the whole thing some common ground with the vocal blues structure described earlier.

Our next example makes use of another, more particular device within the framework of call and response, which is to jump between the higher register and middle register of the piano. This is reminiscent of the great tenor saxophonist Eddie Harris, who, in his both funky and sophisticated manner, might leap in short order between extreme highs and lows.

EXAMPLE 2

The concept is simple, but it can provide a bit of a technical workout if our lines of diverse register are played close together in time. It forces us to get our bearings quickly in another place on the keyboard – to find the notes we mean to play, and to move our hand efficiently and accurately for clean transitions.

This back-and-forth range-jumping idea can be applied to a tune with more chord changes and a swinging rhythm, besides the groovy two-chord vamp setting we have here. Still, it's probably a good effect to use sparingly, lest it become too much of a gimmick in our playing.

Call and response was a prominent feature of the musical environment that helped to form the jazz style and continues to appear throughout the tradition in compositions and in solo statements. See if you can recognize it when you hear it used in obvious or subtle ways. Perhaps you'll want to introduce such a conversational element into your own improvisation.

–Paul Silbergleit

LESSON #92: JUMPING TRACKS

In this lesson, we look at how patterned scale practice can be applied to changing chords in a process that might serve as further exercise, but may also yield musical results that we consider "keepers" for our improvisational approach.

First, let's consider a couple of common ways that jazz musicians play their scales in patterns in order to gain technical control beyond the straight-up-and-down method. For the purpose of this lesson, we'll label these "Pattern 1" and "Pattern 2," although there are many possible variations of this scalar practice regimen.

In Pattern 1, we play through the scale in groups of four consecutive descending notes, starting with the tonic, and doing the same thing from each next tone downward. Here's how it looks on a C major scale, within a limited range:

PATTERN 1

Realize that we could go further with this pattern or play it in reverse, in different ways – moving the group of descending notes up through the scale or using groups of four ascending notes, etc. Many permutations are possible, including the use of smaller or larger note groups. Try coming up with some of these on your own.

Pattern 2 is one that involves a change of direction within each grouping. It could be described as "up one step in the scale, up one more step in the scale, and back down a 3rd interval to the starting note," with that whole unit moving up stepwise through the scale. Notice the word "step" here refers to the distance to the next note in the scale, not necessarily a whole step. Here's how it sounds in C major:

PATTERN 2

It can be plenty enough practice material, for starters, to play one-at-a-time through the various scales in our repertoire, using different up-and-down patterns such as these. But here's the clincher of this lesson, as it pertains to soloing on changes: we'll now try to maintain one of these patterns while shifting to different scales along the way to reflect a particular chord progression.

We'll start with a progression that goes back and forth between two major chords (the maj7#11, to be exact), a half step apart, changing every measure. Here are the scales we'll need:

C Lydian for Cmaj7#11   Db Lydian for Dbmaj7#11

Here's what we get when applying Pattern 1 to these two Lydian scales, for a Cmaj7#11 to D♭maj7#11 progression:

EXAMPLE 1

TRACK 35 0:00 CD 2

Let's try one more application, for the beginning of a B♭ blues progression (B♭7-E♭7-B♭7-B♭7#9 for the first four measures). We'll use these scales:

And we'll run Pattern 2 through them, starting on the tonic B♭. Notice that the only difference between our first two scales is that D becomes D♭ (for E♭7, effectively) – a change that is evident as we hit the second measure:

EXAMPLE 2

TRACK 35 0:12 CD 2

After getting a good handle on basic scales and practicing them with some typical patterns, you can experiment with your own mid-pattern scale-switching and see what works well for certain progressions. At the least, it's a great drill for quickly locating scale tones and, at best, it can lead us to cool new sounds for soloing.

–Paul Silbergleit

THE EXTENSION DIMENSION

The odd-numbered members of a chord beyond the 7th are called its extensions, and focusing on them as a soloist can add a colorful dimension to your playing. In this lesson, we'll try an approach to playing on the upper extensions of a couple of fundamental chord types, along the way taking a look at the scalar origin of each to be clear on what those tones are.

Let's start with the minor 7th chord, using the Dorian scale to derive the full gamut of its tones. (This works better than the natural minor scale by the time we get to the chordal 13th, which will be determined by the scalar 6th.) Here, the tones are numbered for the scale with the idea that we are repeating at the octave, while when enumerating chord tones we keep counting upward. This is how the scale's 6th becomes the chord's 13th, etc., and how Dm7, extended, becomes Dm13.

Realize that the chordal arpeggios resulting from this process are more like lists of chordal members, while in the chord forms we actually play (our chord voicings), they usually have been reordered, often with non-essential tones omitted.

It's good to know, for many purposes, what all the tones of the chords we play really are and to practice them in arpeggio form in different places. But beyond this, we can look at what other chords are found within the arpeggio of the chord in question. There will be several possibilities, but let's note first that from the 5th on up in this Dm13 arpeggio, we have exactly the tones of Am9 – A, C, E, G, and B. (The further up we go, the more we're looking at a chord that sits in the extensions of the original one.)

Now we can test the implications for improv purposes on a Dm7 chord. We'll do this by trying something purely within Am9 chord tones, basically in their own arpeggio form.

EXAMPLE 1

TRACK 36
0:00
CD 2

For a dominant 7th chord, we'll look at the extensions on the unaltered dominant, with nothing flatted or sharped except a ♯11th. This calls for the Lydian dominant scale, which is a Mixolydian (dominant) scale with a raised 4th degree (avoiding the natural 4th or chordal 11th, which could clash with the 3rd). G7 will thus become G13♯11:

Let's again consider the chord-within-the-chord that is rooted on the 5th of the arpeggio, which in this case will be Dm(maj9) (spooky sounding thing with a major 7th in a minor chord), and focus on its arpeggio tones to solo on G7:

EXAMPLE 2

It's also possible to play extensions on the dominant chord that come from a regular Mixolydian scale, which gives us a normal minor 7th chord built on the 5th of the dominant 7th. The chordal 11th is then the non-raised 4th of the scale, which can clash with the 3rd, but within that arpeggio from the 5th it can imply the sound of a suspended chord, or of a ii-V chord pair (as if, in this case, Dm7 were the ii and G7 were the V).

For major 7th chords, a Lydian scale will give us the fully extended maj13♯11, here again avoiding the clashing 4th/11th that was in the more obvious scale (major). We can find a maj9 arpeggio from its 5th.

We need the right scale for each chord, of course, and the system may seem less clear for certain chord types, especially those that have been altered after the fact. (For altered dominants, consider where all those sharped and flatted tones may be, whether or not they fit neatly into new arpeggios.) But experiments in staying up among the extensions, wherever we can find them, can yield interesting new possibilities for our improvisation.

–Paul Silbergleit

LESSON #94: SEQUENTIAL ESSENTIALS

Sequential chords are frequently heard in jazz tunes, in which there are several of the same kind of chord – or pair or small group of chords – in a row, moving around to different roots or keys.

Sometimes this is obvious enough, with a row of dominant 7th chords, for example, moving up or down in a patterned way, like so:

Sometimes it's a little more involved, and maybe trickier to recognize. Consider the following progression:

In this case, what's moving down in sequence is a pair of chords: a ii-V formation (a full ii-V-I chord movement in the key of Bb would be Cm7-F7-Bbmaj7, and here in our first measure we have everything but the I chord). The next measures each have a minor 7th and dominant 7th pair, related to each other in the same way (which may be clear if you sound them out on the keyboard), until these changes resolve to Gm7. So the ii-V is moving as a unit, first down a step, then down a half step, and then a tritone away (three whole steps, either up or down arriving at the same chords by name).

When trying to solo on the progression, this seems like a lot of moving around in short time, especially at fast tempos. But in getting started, the good news is that, since we have the same kind of chords repeatedly, we can focus on some things to play just for those two chords and practice moving them around to different keys as needed. In this way, sequential progressions present a nice opportunity for clearly targeted practice. It may be simpler where we have only one chord type, or are moving the same distance each time. But in reality, the chords of the ii-V pair are so related and intertwined that it's more like finding things to play on just one chord for this sequence. And then comes the part about aiming for these different harmonic areas...

To give this a whirl, let's look at some sample ideas for a one-bar ii-V on Cm7-F7. Notice that each of these melodic cells would sound fine on either Cm7 or F7 alone. We'll call them Ideas 1, 2, and 3, just for reference. These traditional phrases use C Dorian tones and outline the chords, all with a sense of swing.

Next, let's take each of these and move it through the progression, transposing it for each new ii-V.

EXAMPLE 1

TRACK 37
0:00

CD 2

Idea 1:

Idea 2:

Idea 3:

Sometimes this kind of repetition through the changes can sound cool just by itself, but to finish our process we should mix it up a bit. Try going through the progression again, for each ii-V hitting one of these phrases, in the right place for the right chords, but not the same idea each time. It might go something like this (with just a little rhythmic variation leading into Gm7 at the end):

EXAMPLE 2

TRACK 37
0:33

CD 2

Mixing Ideas 1, 2 & 3:

In the long run, we'll do best with a bigger vocabulary of ideas to draw from, as well as allowing ourselves to modify their rhythm, content, and range as we go. This sort of sequential practice helps us to start building that vocabulary and to quickly find where we want to be on the keyboard as the chords to the song move along.

–Paul Silbergleit

LESSON #95: THE TROUBLE WITH SCALES

"What scale do you use to play on this?" is a common question asked by those seeking to learn improvisation. It's an understandable one, as we feel the need to have something to go by – a sure formula of some kind, when approaching this art of infinite possibilities. And indeed, we should learn our scales well. There is much helpful information to be had in relating their tones to particular chords. We can then be equipped with a tool for getting started in many harmonic situations.

The trouble is, scales do not tell the whole story when it comes to improvising – not even about note choice. They can initially free us up by giving us a place to start that at least doesn't sound bad, but then trap us into a box of limitations if we consider any one scale to be the total "how-to" of playing on a certain chord or progression. Here, we'll take a look at a couple of examples of how this may be the case, considering a few common scalar approaches to a dominant 7th chord, with some musical ideas that may or may not follow those guidelines.

For a natural dominant 7th chord – i.e., one without alterations such as a ♭9th, a ♯9th, or ♯5th – a pretty clear answer to the question of scale might be the dominant, or Mixolydian scale, which is the one that is said to generate this chord (through the use of its 1st, 3rd, 5th, and 7th tones, etc.). Another popular way to go about improvising on the dominant 7th is to be less concerned with specific chord content and just play from the blues scale, especially if it's the tonic (I chord) in a blues form or the basis for a one-chord vamp. (This scale may be used throughout the blues form, but its first tone would be the root of the I chord, or the tonic of the key.)

The tones of these two scales are shown here on C, continuing through two octaves (or a little beyond):

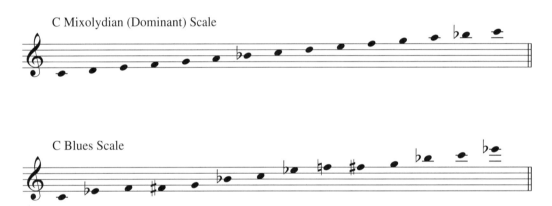

Now here are a couple of phrases that could be played on C7. They would sound normal enough in a jazzer's vocabulary:

EXAMPLE 1

TRACK 38
0:00
CD 2

In both these cases, we have some bluesy flavor, as well as clear reference to chord tones, including the note E, the major 3rd of C7. This could be described in terms of a mix of the C blues and C Mixolydian scales, neither of which would by itself contain all the notes in either line. Notice that there's some scalar overlap here, since the 1st (root), 5th, and 7th tones of the dominant scale or 7th chord – C, G, and B♭ in this case – are also present in the blues scale (Remember that D♯, which begins the second idea, is the enharmonic equivalent of E♭.)

An alternative to the Mixolydian scale, for fitting a natural dominant chord, could be the Lydian dominant scale, or the Mixolydian with a raised 4th degree, which avoids the potential clash of the natural 4th sustained against the chord (and also accommodates a ♯11th, the lone alteration that'll fit in with this type of dominant 7th).

Consider now the following pair of ideas for C7 improvisation:

EXAMPLE 2

TRACK 38
0:24
CD 2

Again, we have lines that could be described as a mix of two scales – this time the Mixolydian and the Lydian dominant – which are both quite specific to the chord. The difference here is only the use of the natural versus raised 4th (F vs. F♯), but if you try substituting one of these notes for the other within either of these phrases, you might find that its character changes quite a bit in terms of natural melodic flow, or how it sits with the C7 chord. Both those notes are used purposefully in both phrases. This would never happen if we stuck strictly to one suggested scale or the other.

The main point is not that scales are unhelpful to the improviser, but that what ultimately rules the day are musical ideas, whether or not they can be summarized by any single scale (other than the chromatic scale, which contains all 12 tones we're working with). Ideally, scales help us find the notes and melodies we hear in our mind's ear by clarifying relationships between tones, both in theory and on the keyboard, as well as by pure sound. If exploration of a scale leads us to discover new combinations that we like and that stick with us in our imagination, that's all well and good to, as long as we don't mistake it for the ultimate "how-to"!

–Paul Silbergleit

LESSON #96: MODES IN JAZZ

If we play a diatonic C major scale over a Cmaj7 chord, the sound you hear is an Ionian major mode. I call modes the "sound you hear" because one scale can create different modes or sounds. Try this first example of C major Ionian, and we'll discuss this more the further we get into the lesson.

EXAMPLE 1

The C major scale has no sharps or flats, and so it is with the D Dorian minor scale. Since both these sounds come from the same notes, what determines the difference? The answer is the chord or bass note being played in the background. What you have in the background affects the way the notes sound. Try this D Dorian minor line.

EXAMPLE 2

Using the notes from the C major scale again, we are creating a new mode called E Phrygian minor. This is a very popular Spanish sound, and you hear it in Latin jazz all the time. Remember, this is the C major scale over E minor. I don't want to confuse you with technical stuff, but the scale degrees based on E would be (1♭2♭3-4-5♭6♭7).

EXAMPLE 3

This is the F Lydian mode; I love the sound of this. It's a fine way to break up the monotony of hearing only the Ionian major scale for a major chord sound. Just remember this is the C major scale over an F major type chord.

EXAMPLE 4

The Mixolydian sound is great for blues and Latin music. Always remember the notes are from the C major scale over a G dominant 7th type chord.

EXAMPLE 5

This is the pure natural minor sound. The A natural minor or Aeolian mode is very common and needs to be used. When students say they're tired of hearing the A minor pentatonic scale, I show them this first. It sounds great with any music really, but it's a must for the budding rock musician.

EXAMPLE 6

The Locrian mode is really the jazz musician's territory. This is the beginning of the trip through the world of the avant-garde jazz and modern dissonant sounds. Get used to hearing this, and you'll be on the way to playing melodies over unusual altered chords.

EXAMPLE 7

With modern jazz comes a serious study. Unless you're prepared to put in the work to know what the possibilities are and what other musicians have done, these new sounds are hard to implement. Work diligently and don't give up.

–John Heussenstamm

Through the study of the blues, I found this concept of switching from a minor pentatonic sound (1♭3-4-5♭7) to the Mixolydian mode, which is sometimes described as a diatonic major scale with a ♭7th (1-2-3-4-5-6♭7). You can use these two sounds over one dominant chord – in this case, we'll use A7. I call the effect of the minor pentatonic bluesy and the Mixolydian jazzy. It's good to have options, and the goal is to be able to switch scales in the middle of a passage without a chord change.

EXAMPLE 1

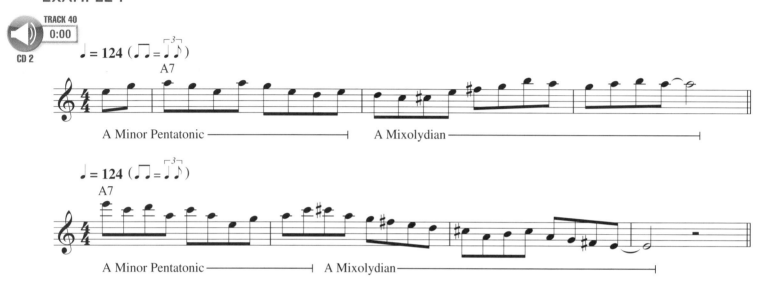

Here I do an extended descending run using the Mixolydian mode first and then finish with a minor pentatonic blues riff.

EXAMPLE 2

Here I begin with an ascending Mixolydian line and return with a descending pentatonic line.

EXAMPLE 3

To capitalize on a melodic idea is important in music. Just think of what Beethoven did with the four-note motive that opens his Symphony No. 5. The first phrase in this example is the springboard for the rest of the exercise. Remember that all this is to be played over A7 or any A dominant chord (A11, A9, A13, etc.).

EXAMPLE 4

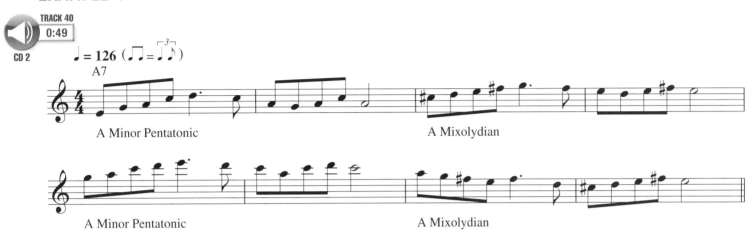

The overlap where two scales fall into the same place is important to study. I've given a few examples below, but try and complete the rest of this study on your own. Notice where the root notes land as a point of reference. The Roman numerals represent what degree of the scale the fingering/pattern begins on.

EXAMPLE 5

–John Heussenstamm

LESSON #98: MANY SCALES OVER ONE CHORD

Without a doubt, the most significant musical application in jazz is the use of scales and modes over dominant 7th type chords. The flexibility one has seems limitless. Once that ♭7th note is introduced in a chord, we have all kinds of options as to which type of scale or sound we wish to use. A lot of a person's style and identification will be based on this fact. Virtuoso guitarist Joe Pass said he always tried to use the ♭5, ♯5, ♭9, and ♯9 notes in all his improvisations over dominant chords. My question is, "How can he do it and get away with it?" Dominant 7th chords can have all these altered notes added to them (G7♭5, G7♯5, G7♭9, G7♯9, G7♭5♭9, etc.). In blues, we hear players using a minor pentatonic scale over a dominant 7th chord. We could explain this with volumes of written materials, but hopefully your ears will discover this reality. These examples have various scales or modes being used over one type of chord: G7.

MIXOLYDIAN

This can also be thought of as the C major scale over G7.

MIXOLYDIAN/IONIAN (BEBOP DOMINANT SCALE)

This has the natural or major 7th as well as the ♭7th and was a favorite of jazz saxophonist Charlie Parker.

DORIAN

This can also be thought of as the F major scale.

PHRYGIAN

This can be thought of as the E♭ major scale.

AEOLIAN

This can be thought of as the B♭ major scale.

MINOR PENTATONIC

This is used extensively in blues.

MAJOR PENTATONIC

This one is used in blues and country.

DIMINISHED

All jazz musicians need to get command of this sound. There could be a place for this in practically every jazz tune. Don't overuse this scale, but you should definitely master it.

COMBO

Jazz can have combinations of scales and sounds running into each other to an endless degree. As you distinguish these scales from one another, you'll be able to apply them wherever and whenever you like.

–John Heussenstamm

LESSON #99: DOMINANT CHORD? MELODIC MINOR

For the blues musician who wants to break into jazz, this is probably the most exciting stage. To hear jazzy sounding lines in the blues is a desire that many musicians have. Not all pianists feel that this should be done, and from the purist's standpoint, it shouldn't. You either stick to the blues riffs or you don't. However, we're talking about jazz here, and jazz is the direction we're heading in.

The A melodic minor scale is simply the A major scale with a ♭3rd or minor 3rd: 1-2-♭3-4-5-6-7. The same harmonic applications fit the melodic minor scale. Let's look at a harmonized A melodic minor scale in 7th chords:

i	ii^ø	♭III+	IV	V	vi^ø	vii^ø
Am(maj7)	Bm7♭5	Cmaj7+	D7	E7	F#m7♭5	G#m7♭5

Remember, these chords were created from the A melodic minor scale.

EXAMPLE 1

The A♭7, D7, and E7 dominant chords are all found in the A melodic minor scale.

EXAMPLE 2

In Example 3, we're hearing a standard change in music: A7 used as our I to a D7 used as a IV. I started with a blues riff over the A7 chord, but then continued with the A melodic minor scale over the D7. This gives you an effect that makes the style more like jazz than straight-ahead blues.

EXAMPLE 3

Here we're using some standard changes found in practically all styles of blues, jazz, and pop music to demonstrate the effective quality of the melodic minor scale for jazz purposes. In some books and articles I've seen, they even call it the "jazz minor scale." Over the top of the E7 and D7 chords, I'm using only the A melodic minor scale.

EXAMPLE 4

The second line over the A7 chord is a blues riff constructed using the A Mixolydian scale. It also has a blue note (the #9th or ♭3rd). In blues theory, there are rules that let you use minor-sounding notes (♭3rd, ♭5th) over a dominant chord to give the music that bluesy sound. The same train of thought should be used in jazz as well. Most people feel that the best jazz musicians are also excellent blues players. Many educational halls of learning say that a jazz musician should start by studying the blues, and more often than not, that proves to be true.

–John Heussenstamm

LESSON #100: ENCLOSURE TIME

Enclosure is another concept for using notes that might not be in the key you're in. Whether the notes are part of the key or not, this device allows you to come up with some interesting small resolutions. When we use the term "targeting" in music, we mean to say that we've picked out a note that we're aiming for. We basically arrange notes around that targeted note in a way that makes it sound as though we were heading in that direction. The first time I heard about this is when I was studying a Charlie Parker book. These kinds of sounds work really well in bebop or up-tempo swing. I've presented several practical examples in the key of C major. Just remember that we're aiming for notes within the key of C, and this whole reality should become clear. In this first row, we've targeted the C note:

TRACK 43
0:00
CD 2

D is the targeted note:

TRACK 43
0:20
CD 2

G is the targeted note:

TRACK 43
0:40
CD 2

In this next example, I'm going to use a basic C major arpeggio and build a line using enclosures. With each following exercise, we'll pick a different chord to help demonstrate this concept. Creating lines that sound like jazz is a question that gets put to me in many lessons with jazz students. To get that bebop sound in jazz, the enclosure is one sure way.

EXAMPLE 1

TRACK 43
1:00
CD 2

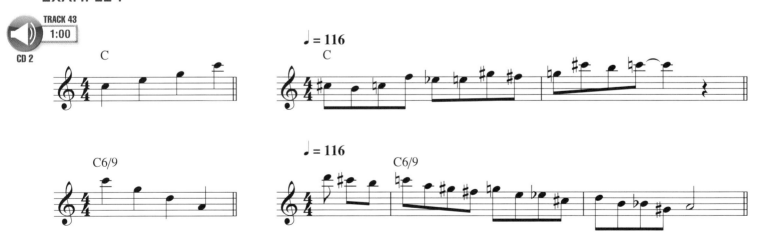

This chord uses a ♭7th. I'm also going to use a different enclosure for each note instead of a repetitive sequence. To me, this is the breakaway point from conservative thinking to the jazz musician's approach.

EXAMPLE 2

When you combine enclosures with modern altered chords/arpeggios, you really have cracked the nutshell. Getting used to these sounds requires a lot of listening and practicing. There are endless ways to incorporate enclosures.

EXAMPLE 3

As I say in many of my lessons, you should try and come up with some of your own stuff. Study players like Charlie Parker and find passages where he used these enclosure concepts. Jazz is a language that needs contributions to keep it fresh and up-and-running.

–John Heussenstamm

PLAY PIANO LIKE A PRO!

AMAZING PHRASING – KEYBOARD
50 Ways to Improve Your Improvisational Skills
by Debbie Denke

Amazing Phrasing is for any keyboard player interested in learning how to improvise and how to improve their creative phrasing. This method is divided into three parts: melody, harmony, and rhythm & style. The companion CD contains 44 full-band demos for listening, as well as many play-along examples so you can practice improvising over various musical styles and progressions.
00842030 Book/CD Pack $16.95

BEBOP LICKS FOR PIANO
A Dictionary of Melodic Ideas for Improvisation
by Les Wise

Written for the musician who is interested in acquiring a firm foundation for playing jazz, this unique book/CD pack presents over 800 licks. By building up a vocabulary of these licks, players can connect them together in endless possibilities to form larger phrases and complete solos. The book includes piano notation, and the CD contains helpful note-for-note demos of every lick.
00311854 Book/CD Pack $16.99

BOOGIE WOOGIE FOR BEGINNERS
by Frank Paparelli

A short easy method for learning to play boogie woogie, designed for the beginner and average pianist. Includes: exercises for developing left-hand bass • 25 popular boogie woogie bass patterns • arrangements of "Down the Road a Piece" and "Answer to the Prayer" by well-known pianists • a glossary of musical terms for dynamics, tempo and style.
00120517 .... $7.95

INTROS, ENDINGS & TURNAROUNDS FOR KEYBOARD
Essential Phrases for Swing, Latin, Jazz Waltz, and Blues Styles
by John Valerio

Learn the intros, endings and turnarounds that all of the pros know and use! This new keyboard instruction book by John Valerio covers swing styles, ballads, Latin tunes, jazz waltzes, blues, major and minor keys, vamps and pedal tones, and more.
00290525 .... $12.95

JAZZ PIANO VOICINGS
An Essential Resource for Aspiring Jazz Musicians
by Rob Mullins

The jazz idiom can often appear mysterious and difficult for musicians who were trained to play other types of music. Long-time performer and educator Rob Mullins helps players enter the jazz world by providing voicings that will help the player develop skills in the jazz genre and start sounding professional right away – without years of study! Includes a "Numeric Voicing Chart," chord indexes in all 12 keys, info about what range of the instrument you play chords in, and a beginning approach to bass lines.
00310914 .... $19.95

101 KEYBOARD TIPS
Stuff All the Pros Know and Use
by Craig Weldon

Ready to take your keyboard playing to the next level? This book will show you how. *101 Keyboard Tips* presents valuable how-to insight that players of all styles and levels can benefit from. The text, photos, music, diagrams and accompanying CD provide an essential, easy-to-use resource for a variety of topics, including: techniques, improvising and soloing, equipment, practicing, ear training, performance, theory, and much more.
00310933 Book/CD Pack $14.95

OSCAR PETERSON – JAZZ EXERCISES, MINUETS, ETUDES & PIECES FOR PIANO

Legendary jazz pianist Oscar Peterson has long been devoted to the education of piano students. In this book he offers dozens of pieces designed to empower the student, whether novice or classically trained, with the technique needed to become an accomplished jazz pianist.
00311225 .... $12.99

PIANO AEROBICS
by Wayne Hawkins

Piano Aerobics is a set of exercises that introduces students to many popular styles of music, including jazz, salsa, swing, rock, blues, new age, gospel, stride, and bossa nova. In addition, there is a CD with accompaniment tracks featuring professional musicians playing in those styles.
00311863 Book/CD Pack $19.99

PIANO FITNESS
A Complete Workout
by Mark Harrison

This book will give you a thorough technical workout, while having fun at the same time! The accompanying CD allows you to play along with a rhythm section as you practice your scales, arpeggios, and chords in all keys. Instead of avoiding technique exercises because they seem too tedious or difficult, you'll look forward to playing them. Various voicings and rhythmic settings, which are extremely useful in a variety of pop and jazz styles, are also introduced.
00311995 Book/CD Pack $19.99

THE TOTAL KEYBOARD PLAYER
A Complete Guide to the Sounds, Styles & Sonic Spectrum
by Dave Adler

Do you play the keyboards in your sleep? Do you live for the feel of the keys beneath your fingers? If you answered in the affirmative, then read on, brave musical warrior! All you seek is here: the history, the tricks, the stops, the patches, the plays, the holds, the fingering, the dynamics, the exercises, the magic. Everything you always wanted to know about keyboards, all in one amazing key-centric compendium.
00311977 Book/CD Pack $19.99

HAL•LEONARD®
7777 W. BLUEMOUND RD. P.O. BOX 13819
MILWAUKEE, WISCONSIN 53213

www.halleonard.com

Prices, contents, and availability subject to change without notice.

Expand Your Jazz Piano Technique

BLUES, JAZZ & ROCK RIFFS FOR KEYBOARDS
by William T. Eveleth
Because so much of today's popular music has its roots in blues, the material included here is a vital component of jazz, rock, R&B, gospel, soul, and even pop. The author has compiled actual licks, riffs, turnaround phrases, embellishments, and basic patterns that define good piano blues and can be used as a basis for players to explore and create their own style.
00221028 Book...$9.95

BOOGIE WOOGIE FOR BEGINNERS
by Frank Paparelli
This bestseller is now available with a CD of demonstration tracks! A short easy method for learning to play boogie woogie, designed for the beginner and average pianist. Includes: exercises for developing left-hand bass; 25 popular boogie woogie bass patterns; arrangements of "Down the Road a Piece" and "Answer to the Prayer" by well-known pianists; a glossary of musical terms for dynamics, tempo and style; and more.
00312559 Book/CD Pack $14.99

A CLASSICAL APPROACH TO JAZZ PIANO IMPROVISATION
by Dominic Alldis
This keyboard instruction book is designed for the person who was trained classically but wants to expand into the very exciting — yet very different — world of jazz improvisation. Author Dominic Alldis provides clear explanations and musical examples of: pentatonic improvisation; the blues; rock piano; rhythmic placement; scale theory; major, minor and pentatonic scale theory applications; and more.
00310979 Book.. $16.95

THE HARMONY OF BILL EVANS
by Jack Reilly
A compilation of articles — now revised and expanded — that originally appeared in the quarterly newsletter *Letter from Evans*, this unique folio features extensive analysis of Evans' work. Pieces examined include: B Minor Waltz • Funny Man • How Deep Is the Ocean • I Fall in Love Too Easily • I Should Care • Peri's Scope • Time Remembered • and Twelve Tone Tune.
00699405 Book...$19.99

Prices, contents, and availability subject to change without notice.

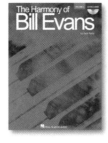

THE HARMONY OF BILL EVANS - VOLUME 2
by Jack Reilly
Reilly's second volume includes two important theory chapters, plus ten of Bill's most passionate and melodically gorgeous works. The accompanying audio CD will add to the enjoyment, understanding, and appreciation of the written examples. Songs include: For Nenette • January • Laurie • Maxine • Song for Helen • Turn Out the Stars • Very Early • Waltz for Debby • and more.
00311828 Book/CD Pack $29.99

AN INTRODUCTION TO JAZZ CHORD VOICING FOR KEYBOARD - 2ND EDITION
by Bill Boyd
This book is designed for the pianist/keyboardist with moderate technical skills and reading ability who desires to play jazz styles and learn to improvise from reading chord symbols. It is an ideal self-teaching book for keyboardists in high school and junior high jazz ensembles. Unique features of this book include chords and progressions written out in all keys, a simple fingering system which applies to all keys, and coverage of improvising and solo playing.
00854100 Book/CD Pack...............................$19.95

INTROS, ENDINGS & TURNAROUNDS FOR KEYBOARD
ESSENTIAL PHRASES FOR SWING, LATIN, JAZZ WALTZ, AND BLUES STYLES
by John Valerio
Learn the intros, endings and turnarounds that all of the pros know and use! This new keyboard instruction book by John Valerio covers swing styles, ballads, Latin tunes, jazz waltzes, blues, major and minor keys, vamps and pedal tones, and more.
00290525 Book $12.95

JAZZ ETUDE INSPIRATIONS
EIGHT PIANO ETUDES INSPIRED BY THE MASTERS
by Jeremy Siskind
Etudes in the style of legendary greats Oscar Peterson, Duke Ellington, McCoy Tyner, Jelly Roll Morton, Chick Corea, Brad Mehldau, Count Basie and Herbie Hancock will help students master some technical challenges posed by each artist's individual style. The performance notes include a biography, practice tips and a list of significant recordings. Tunes include: Count on Me • Hand Battle • Jelly Roll Me Home • Minor Tyner • Oscar's Bounce • Pineapple Woman • Repeat After Me • Tears Falling on Still Water.
00296860 Book...$8.99

JAZZ PIANO
by Liam Noble
Featuring lessons, music, historical analysis and rare photos, this book/CD pack provides a complete overview of the techniques and styles popularized by 15 of the greatest jazz pianists of all time. All the best are here: from the early ragtime stylings of Ferdinand "Jelly Roll" Morton, to the modal escapades of Bill Evans, through the '70s jazz funk of Herbie Hancock. CD contains 15 full-band tracks.
00311050 Book/CD Pack $17.95

JAZZ PIANO CONCEPTS & TECHNIQUES
by John Valerio
This book provides a step-by-step approach to learning basic piano realizations of jazz and pop tunes from lead sheets. Systems for voicing chords are presented from the most elementary to the advanced along with methods for practicing each system. Both the non-jazz and the advanced jazz player will benefit from the focus on: chords, chord voicings, harmony, melody and accompaniment, and styles.
00290490 Book $16.95

JAZZ PIANO TECHNIQUE
by John Valerio
This one-of-a-kind book applies traditional technique exercises to specific jazz piano needs. Topics include: scales (major, minor, chromatic, pentatonic, etc.), arpeggios (triads, seventh chords, upper structures), finger independence exercises (static position, held notes, Hanon exercises), and more! The CD includes 45 recorded examples.
00312059 Book/CD Pack..............................$19.99

JAZZ PIANO VOICINGS
by Rob Mullins
Long-time performer and educator Rob Mullins helps players enter the jazz world by providing voicings that will help the player develop skills in the jazz genre and start sounding professional right away — without years of study! Includes a "Numeric Voicing Chart," chord indexes in all 12 keys, info about what range of the instrument you can play chords in, and a beginning approach to bass lines.
00310914 Book...................................$19.95

HAL•LEONARD® CORPORATION
7777 W. BLUEMOUND RD. P.O. BOX 13819 MILWAUKEE, WI 53213
www.halleonard.com
1213

jazz piano solos series

Each volume features exciting new arrangements
of the songs which helped define a style.

vol. 1 miles davis
00306521..............................$15.99

vol. 2 jazz blues
00306522..............................$15.99

vol. 3 latin jazz
00310621..............................$15.99

vol. 4 bebop jazz
00310709..............................$15.99

vol. 5 cool jazz
00310710..............................$15.99

vol. 6 hard bop
00310711..............................$15.99

vol. 7 smooth jazz
00310727..............................$15.99

vol. 8 jazz pop
00311786..............................$15.99

vol. 9 duke ellington
00311787..............................$15.99

vol. 10 jazz ballads
00311788..............................$15.99

vol. 11 soul jazz
00311789..............................$15.99

vol. 12 swinging jazz
00311797..............................$15.99

vol. 13 jazz gems
00311899..............................$15.99

vol. 14 jazz classics
00311900..............................$15.99

vol. 15 bossa nova
00311906..............................$15.99

vol. 16 disney
00312121..............................$16.99

vol. 17 antonio carlos jobim
00312122..............................$15.99

vol. 18 modern jazz quartet
00307270..............................$16.99

vol. 19 bill evans
00307273..............................$16.99

vol. 20 gypsy jazz
00307289..............................$16.99

vol. 21 new orleans jazz piano solos
00312169..............................$16.99

vol. 22 classic jazz
00001529..............................$16.99

vol. 23 jazz for lovers
00312548..............................$16.99

vol. 25 christmas songs
00101790..............................$16.99

vol. 26 george gershwin
00103353..............................$16.99

vol. 27 late night jazz
00312547..............................$16.99

HAL•LEONARD® CORPORATION
7777 W. BLUEMOUND RD. P.O. BOX 13819 MILWAUKEE, WI 53213

www.halleonard.com

Prices, contents and availability subject to change without notice.

0813